FAVORITE BRAND NAME

FESTIVE

HOLIDAY COOKIES

PUBLICATIONS INTERNATIONAL, LTD.

Front and back cover photography and photography on pages 7, 19, 23, 35, 41, 59, 73, 77 and 89 by Sanders Studios, Inc., Chicago.

Pictured on the front cover: Cherry Coconut Cookies *(page 34)*, Cherry Rum Cookies *(page 22)*, Chocolate Scotcheroos *(page 88)*, Chocolate Thumbprints *(page 36)*, Corn Flake Macaroons *(page 25)*, Cream Cheese Cookies *(page 34)*, Double Crunch Biscotti *(page 6)*, Frosted Butter Cookies *(page 40)*, Frosty Cherry Cookies *(page 9)*, Lemon Pecan Crescents *(page 21)*, Peanut Butter Stars *(page 18)*, Pecan Crunchies *(page 72)*, Peppermint Refrigerator Slices *(page 20)*, Snickerdoodles *(page 72)*, Snow Puff Cookies *(page 9)*, Spicy Pumpkin Cookies *(page 58)* and Spritz Christmas Trees *(page 18)*.

ISBN: 0-7853-0465-7
Manufactured in U.S.A.

8 7 6 5 4 3 2 1

Microwave Cooking: Microwave ovens vary in wattage. The microwave cooking times given in this publication are approximate. Use the cooking times as guidelines and check for doneness before adding more time. Consult manufacturer's instructions for suitable microwave-safe cooking dishes.

FAVORITE BRAND NAME

FESTIVE HOLIDAY COOKIES

Holiday Specialties

▲ ▲ ▲

DOUBLE CRUNCH BISCOTTI

⅓ cup vegetable oil
¾ cup sugar
3 eggs, beaten
½ teaspoon almond extract
½ teaspoon vanilla extract
2½ cups all-purpose flour
2 cups ALMOND DELIGHT®
  Brand Cereal, crushed to
  1 cup

2 teaspoons baking powder
12 ounces chocolate, melted
  (optional)
¼ cup chopped almonds
  (optional)

Preheat oven to 350°F. Lightly grease cookie sheet. In large bowl, combine oil and sugar. Beat in eggs, almond extract and vanilla. Gradually stir in flour, cereal and baking powder. Divide dough in half. Place each half of dough on prepared cookie sheet, shaping each into a 3½-inch by 11-inch log. Bake 25 to 28 minutes or until lightly browned. Remove from oven; immediately cut into ½-inch-thick slices. Place slices, cut side down, on clean ungreased cookie sheet. Bake 13 minutes, turning cookies over after 8 minutes. Cool on wire rack. If desired, spread chocolate on one end of each cookie; sprinkle with almonds. *Makes 44 cookies*

Top to bottom: Frosty Cherry Cookies (page 9),
Double Crunch Biscotti, Snow Puff Cookies (page 9)

ALMOND CREAM COOKIES

¾ cup (1½ sticks) margarine, softened
¾ cup granulated sugar
½ cup plus 2 tablespoons soft-style cream cheese
1 egg
1 teaspoon almond extract
1¼ cups all-purpose flour

¾ cup QUAKER® Corn Meal
½ teaspoon baking powder
½ cup coarsely chopped almonds
1 cup powdered sugar
1 tablespoon milk or water
Red or green candied cherries

Preheat oven to 350°F. Beat margarine, granulated sugar and ½ cup cream cheese at medium speed of electric mixer until fluffy. Add egg and almond extract; mix until well blended. Gradually add combined flour, corn meal and baking powder; mix well. Stir in almonds. Drop by rounded teaspoonfuls onto ungreased cookie sheet. Bake 12 to 14 minutes or until edges are golden brown. Cool on cookie sheet for 2 minutes; remove to wire rack. Cool completely.

Mix remaining 2 tablespoons cream cheese and powdered sugar until blended. Add milk; mix until smooth. Spread over cookies. Garnish with halved red or green candied cherries, if desired. Store tightly covered.

Makes about 4 dozen cookies

Almond Cream Cookies

FROSTY CHERRY COOKIES

½ cup (1 stick) butter or
   margarine
1 cup plus 3 tablespoons
   sugar, divided
1 egg, slightly beaten
½ teaspoon almond extract
1½ cups all-purpose flour

½ teaspoon salt
½ teaspoon baking soda
½ teaspoon baking powder
2 cups Rice CHEX® brand
   cereal, crushed to 1 cup
½ cup chopped green and red
   glacé cherries

Preheat oven to 350°F. In large bowl, combine butter and 1 cup sugar. Stir in egg and almond extract. Stir in flour, salt, baking soda and baking powder; mix well. Stir in cereal and cherries. Shape into ¾-inch balls. In small bowl, place remaining 3 tablespoons sugar. Roll balls in sugar. Place, 2 inches apart, on baking sheet. Bake 8 to 10 minutes or until bottoms are lightly browned.   *Makes 6 dozen cookies*

SNOW PUFF COOKIES

1 cup (2 sticks) butter or
   margarine, softened
1 cup sifted confectioners'
   sugar
2 teaspoons vanilla

2 cups all-purpose flour
1 cup Wheat CHEX® brand
   cereal, crushed to ⅓ cup
½ teaspoon salt
Confectioners' sugar

Preheat oven to 325°F. In large bowl, combine butter and 1 cup sugar until well blended. Stir in vanilla. Stir in flour, cereal and salt, mixing well. Shape into 1-inch balls. Place, 2 inches apart, on ungreased baking sheet. Bake 14 to 16 minutes or until bottoms are lightly browned. Cool. Roll in confectioners' sugar.   *Makes 3 dozen cookies*

CHOCOLATE-DIPPED ALMOND HORNS

1½ cups powdered sugar
1 cup butter or margarine, softened
2 egg yolks
1½ teaspoons vanilla
2 cups all-purpose flour

½ cup ground almonds
1 teaspoon cream of tartar
1 teaspoon baking soda
1 cup semisweet chocolate chips, melted
Additional powdered sugar

Preheat oven to 325°F. Combine 1½ cups powdered sugar and butter in large bowl. Beat at medium speed with electric mixer until creamy. Add egg yolks and vanilla: beat until well blended. Add flour, almonds, cream of tartar and baking soda; beat at low speed until well mixed.

Shape dough into 1-inch balls. (If dough is too soft to handle, refrigerate until firm.) Roll into 2-inch-long ropes, tapering both ends. Curve ropes into crescent shapes. Place 2 inches apart on cookie sheets.

Bake 8 to 10 minutes or until set. Cookies do not brown. Remove cookies to wire racks; cool completely. Dip half of each cookie into chocolate; sprinkle remaining half with additional powdered sugar. Refrigerate until set.   *Makes about 3 dozen cookies*

CHERRY DOT COOKIES

2¼ cups all-purpose flour
2 teaspoons baking powder
½ teaspoon salt
¾ cup margarine, softened
1 cup sugar
2 eggs
2 tablespoons skim milk
1 teaspoon vanilla
1 cup chopped nuts

1 cup finely cut pitted dates
⅓ cup finely chopped maraschino cherries
2⅔ cups KELLOGGS'® CORN FLAKES® cereal, crushed to 1⅓ cups
15 maraschino cherries, cut into quarters

1. Preheat oven to 350°F. Stir together flour, baking powder and salt. Set aside.

2. In large mixing bowl, beat margarine and sugar until light and fluffy. Add eggs. Beat well. Stir in milk and vanilla. Add flour mixture. Mix well. Stir in nuts, dates and ⅓ cup chopped cherries.

3. Shape level measuring tablespoons of dough into balls. Roll in Kelloggs'® Corn Flakes® cereal. Place on cookie sheets coated with cooking spray. Top each cookie with cherry quarter.

4. Bake about 12 minutes or until lightly browned.
                                        Makes about 5 dozen cookies

Chocolate-Dipped Almond Horns

HOLIDAY SHORTBREAD WITH VARIATIONS

1 cup (2 sticks) butter	2½ cups all-purpose flour
½ cup sugar	¼ teaspoon salt

Preheat oven to 375°F. Cream butter in large mixer bowl until fluffy. Add sugar; beat until light and fluffy. Gradually blend in flour and salt. Roll out on lightly floured surface to 11×7-inch rectangle, ½ inch thick. Cut into 1-inch squares. Bake on unbuttered cookie sheets 12 to 15 minutes or until a pale golden color. Cool completely on wire racks. Store at room temperature in container with tight fitting lid.   *Makes about 6 dozen*

Variations

Anise Stars: Prepare Basic Shortbread, stirring in ¾ teaspoon anise extract and ¼ teaspoon nutmeg with flour and salt. Wrap dough in plastic wrap. Refrigerate 1 to 2 hours. Roll dough to ¼-inch thickness on lightly floured surface. Cut into star shapes using floured cutter. Bake in preheated 375°F oven on unbuttered cookie sheets 13 to 15 minutes or until very pale golden color. Cool completely on wire racks. Decorate with red and green frosting and small silver dragées. Makes 3 to 4 dozen.

Rum Raisin Balls: Prepare Basic Shortbread, stirring in 1 cup golden seedless raisins and 1 teaspoon rum extract with flour and salt. Form into 1-inch balls. Bake in preheated 375°F oven on unbuttered cookie sheets 15 to 18 minutes or until pale golden color. Remove from cookie sheets; cool completely on wire racks. Dust lightly with confectioners' sugar before serving. Makes 5 dozen.

Noel Tarts: Prepare Basic Shortbread, stirring in 1 teaspoon vanilla extract with flour and salt. Press rounded tablespoonfuls of dough into 1¾-inch muffin cups. Bake in preheated 375°F oven 18 to 20 minutes or until pale golden color. Cool in pan 10 minutes. Carefully remove from pan; cool completely on wire rack. Fill as desired with pie filling, pudding, mincemeat, etc. Makes 3 dozen.

Chocolate-Frosted Almond Bars: Prepare Basic Shortbread, reducing flour to 2 cups. Add ½ cup finely ground almonds and 1 teaspoon almond extract with flour and salt. Press into unbuttered 13×9-inch baking pan. Bake in preheated 375°F oven 20 to 25 minutes or until pale golden color. Cool completely in pan on wire rack. Frost with 1 package (6 ounces) semisweet chocolate morsels, melted, and combined with ½ cup dairy sour cream and 1 teaspoon vanilla extract. Cut into bars. Decorate with sliced almonds. Makes 4 dozen.

Favorite recipe from **American Dairy Association**

Top to bottom: Anise Stars, Rum Raisin Balls, Noel Tarts, Chocolate-Frosted Almond Bars

DOUBLE SURPRISE COOKIES

2/3 cup butter or margarine
1/3 cup sugar
2 egg yolks
1/2 teaspoon vanilla
1/8 teaspoon almond extract
1 1/2 cups all-purpose flour
1/4 teaspoon salt
36 "M&M's®" Peanut, Peanut
    Butter or Almond
    Chocolate Candies

1/4 cup confectioners'
    (powdered) sugar
1 1/2 teaspoons water
3/4 cup "M&M's®" Semi-Sweet
    Chocolate Candies*

Preheat oven to 350°F. In mixer, beat butter 30 seconds. Gradually add sugar; beat until light and fluffy. Add egg yolks, vanilla and almond extract; beat thoroughly. Stir together flour and salt. Add to creamed mixture; mix well. Cover and chill at least 1 hour. For each cookie, shape, with floured hands, a rounded teaspoonful dough around each Peanut, Peanut Butter or Almond "M&M's®" to form a ball, about 1 inch in diameter. Place, 1 inch apart, on ungreased baking sheet. Bake 12 to 15 minutes until dough springs back when touched and cookie is lightly browned on bottom. Remove to wire rack; cool completely. To decorate, mix together confectioners' sugar and water until smooth. Spread on tops of cookies; immediately sprinkle generously with "M&M's®" Semi-Sweet Chocolate Candies, pressing in lightly.   *Makes 36 cookies*

*Found in baking section.

PEPPERMINT MACAROONS

2 egg whites
1 cup sugar
2 cups KELLOGGS'® SPECIAL
    K® cereal
1/2 cup (about 4 ounces)
    peppermint candy canes,
    crushed (about 5 candy
    canes)

1/2 teaspoon vanilla
Vegetable cooking spray

1. In the bowl of an electric mixer, beat egg whites until foamy. Gradually add sugar, beating until stiff and glossy.

2. Add Kelloggs'® Special K® cereal, crushed candy canes and vanilla, mixing until blended. Drop by rounded teaspoonfuls onto baking sheets lightly coated with cooking spray.

3. Bake at 350°F about 12 minutes. Remove immediately from baking sheets. Let cool on wire racks. Store in airtight container.
                              Makes about 3 1/2 dozen cookies

Kolacky

KOLACKY

½ cup butter or margarine,
　softened
3 ounces cream cheese,
　softened
1 teaspoon vanilla
1 cup all-purpose flour

⅛ teaspoon salt
6 teaspoons fruit preserves,
　assorted flavors
1 egg
1 teaspoon cold water
Powdered sugar (optional)

Combine butter and cream cheese in large bowl; beat until smooth and creamy. Blend in vanilla. Combine flour and salt; gradually add to butter mixture, mixing until mixture forms soft dough. Divide dough in half; wrap each half in plastic wrap. Refrigerate until firm.

Preheat oven to 375°F. Roll out half of dough on lightly floured pastry cloth or board to ⅛-inch thickness. Cut with top of glass or biscuit cutter into 3-inch rounds. Spoon ½ teaspoon preserves onto center of each dough circle. Beat egg with water; lightly brush onto edges of dough circles. Bring three edges of dough up over fruit spread; pinch edges together to seal. Place on ungreased cookie sheets; brush with egg mixture. Repeat with remaining dough, preserves and egg mixture. Bake 12 minutes or until golden brown. Let stand on cookie sheets 1 minute; transfer to wire rack. Cool completely. Sprinkle with powdered sugar, if desired. Store in tightly covered container. *Makes 2 dozen*

Anise Cookie Cordials

ANISE COOKIE CORDIALS

2¾ cups all-purpose flour
1½ teaspoons baking powder
1 cup sugar
½ cup butter, softened
3 eggs
2 tablespoons anise-flavored liqueur
2 tablespoons water

1 tablespoon anise seeds
½ of 12-ounce package (1 cup) NESTLÉ® Toll House® Mini Morsels Semi-Sweet Chocolate
1 cup coarsely chopped toasted almonds

In medium bowl, combine flour and baking powder; set aside. In large bowl, combine sugar and butter; beat until creamy. Add eggs, anise-flavored liqueur, water and anise seeds; beat until well blended. Gradually beat in flour mixture. Stir in mini morsels and almonds. Cover; chill several hours.

Preheat oven to 375°F. Divide dough into four pieces. With floured hands, shape each piece into 15½ × 2 × ½-inch loaf. Place loaves, 4 inches apart, on greased cookie sheets. Bake at 375°F for 15 minutes. Remove from oven. Cut into 1-inch slices. Place slices back on cookie sheets. Bake at 375°F for 7 minutes. Turn cookies over. Bake at 375°F for 7 minutes. Cool completely on wire racks.

Makes about 4½ dozen (1-inch) cookies

TWO-TONED SPRITZ COOKIES

1 square (1 ounce)
  unsweetened chocolate,
  coarsely chopped
2¼ cups all-purpose flour
¼ teaspoon salt

1 cup butter or margarine,
  softened
1 cup sugar
1 large egg
1 teaspoon vanilla

Melt chocolate in small, heavy saucepan over low heat, stirring constantly; set aside. Combine flour and salt; set aside. Beat butter and sugar in large bowl until light and fluffy. Beat in egg and vanilla. Gradually add flour mixture. Remove and reserve 2 cups dough. Beat chocolate into dough in bowl until smooth. Cover both doughs and refrigerate until easy to handle, about 20 minutes.

Preheat oven to 400°F. Roll out vanilla dough between two sheets of waxed paper to ½-inch thickness. Cut into 5×4-inch rectangles. Place chocolate dough on sheet of waxed paper. Using waxed paper to hold dough, roll it back and forth to form a log about 1 inch in diameter. Cut into 5-inch-long logs. Place chocolate log in center of vanilla rectangle. Wrap vanilla dough around log and fit into cookie press fitted with star disc. Press dough onto cookie sheets 1½ inches apart. Bake about 10 minutes or until just set. Remove cookies with spatula to wire racks; cool completely.   *Makes about 4 dozen cookies*

LEMON BUTTER COOKIES

2 cups all-purpose flour
½ teaspoon baking soda
1 cup margarine, softened
1 cup sugar

1 teaspoon vanilla extract
1 teaspoon grated lemon peel
1 egg
  Sugar

Preheat oven to 375°F.

In small bowl, combine flour and baking soda; set aside.

In medium bowl, with electric mixer at medium speed, beat margarine, sugar, vanilla and lemon peel just until blended. Beat in egg until light and fluffy. Gradually blend in flour mixture. Drop dough by rounded teaspoonfuls, 2 inches apart, onto ungreased cookie sheets. Grease bottom of small glass; dip into sugar. Press onto dough to flatten slightly. Bake for 8 to 10 minutes. Remove from sheets; cool on wire racks. Store in airtight container.   *Makes about 4½ dozen cookies*

Favorite recipe from **Nabisco Foods Group**

SPRITZ CHRISTMAS TREES

⅓ cup (3½ ounces) almond
    paste
1 egg
¼ cup CRISCO® Oil or
    CRISCO® PURITAN®
    Canola Oil
8 drops green food coloring

1 package DUNCAN HINES®
    Golden Sugar Cookie Mix
1 container DUNCAN HINES®
    Creamy Homestyle
    Vanilla Frosting
Cinnamon candies, for
    garnish

1. Preheat oven to 375°F. Combine almond paste and egg in large bowl. Beat at low speed with electric mixer until blended. Add oil and green food coloring. Beat until smooth and evenly tinted. Add cookie mix. Beat at low speed until thoroughly blended.

2. Fit cookie press with Christmas tree plate; fill with dough. Force dough through press 2 inches apart onto ungreased baking sheets. Bake at 375°F for 6 to 7 minutes or until set but not browned. Cool 1 minute on baking sheets. Remove to cooling racks. Cool completely.

3. To decorate, fill resealable plastic bag half full with vanilla frosting. Do not seal bag. Cut pinpoint hole in bottom corner of bag. Pipe small dot of frosting onto tip of one cookie tree and top with cinnamon candy. Repeat with remaining cookies. Pipe remaining frosting to form garland on cookie trees. Allow frosting to set before storing between layers of waxed paper in airtight container.   *Makes about 6 dozen cookies*

PEANUT BUTTER STARS

1 package DUNCAN HINES®
    Peanut Butter Cookie Mix
1 egg
¼ cup CRISCO® Oil or
    CRISCO® PURITAN®
    Canola Oil

1 package (3½ ounces)
    chocolate sprinkles
1 package (7 ounces) milk
    chocolate candy stars

1. Preheat oven to 375°F.

2. Combine cookie mix, contents of peanut butter packet from Mix, egg and oil in large bowl. Stir until thoroughly blended. Shape dough into 1-inch balls. Roll in chocolate sprinkles. Place 2 inches apart on ungreased baking sheets. Bake at 375°F for 8 to 10 minutes or until set. Immediately place milk chocolate candy stars on top of hot cookies. Cool 1 minute on baking sheets. Remove to cooling racks. Cool completely. Store in airtight containers.   *Makes 4½ to 5 dozen cookies*

*Counter-clockwise from top: Peppermint
Refrigerator Slices (page 20), Lemon Pecan
Crescents (page 21), Spritz Christmas Trees,
Peanut Butter Stars*

PEPPERMINT REFRIGERATOR SLICES

¾ cup CRISCO® Oil or
    CRISCO® PURITAN®
    Canola Oil, divided
3 eggs, divided
3 to 4 drops red food
    coloring

¾ teaspoon peppermint
    extract, divided
3 packages DUNCAN HINES®
    Golden Sugar Cookie Mix,
    divided
3 to 4 drops green food
    coloring

1. **For pink cookie dough,** combine ¼ cup oil, one egg, red food coloring and ¼ teaspoon peppermint extract in large bowl. Stir until evenly tinted. Add one cookie mix and stir until thoroughly blended.

2. **For green cookie dough,** combine ¼ cup oil, one egg, green food coloring and ¼ teaspoon peppermint extract in large bowl. Stir until evenly tinted. Add one cookie mix and stir until thoroughly blended.

3. **For plain cookie dough,** combine remaining cookie mix, ¼ cup oil, egg and ¼ teaspoon peppermint extract in large bowl. Stir until thoroughly blended.

4. **To assemble,** divide each batch of cookie dough into four equal portions. Shape each portion into 12-inch-long roll on waxed paper. Lay one pink roll beside one green roll; press together slightly. Place one plain roll on top. Press rolls together to form one tri-colored roll; wrap in waxed paper or plastic wrap. Repeat with remaining rolls to form three more tri-colored rolls; wrap separately in waxed paper or plastic wrap. Refrigerate rolls for several hours or overnight.

5. Preheat oven to 375°F.

6. Cut chilled rolls into ¼-inch-thick slices. Place 2 inches apart on ungreased baking sheets. Bake at 375°F for 7 to 8 minutes or until set but not browned. Cool 1 minute on baking sheets. Remove to cooling racks. Cool completely. Store in airtight containers.

Makes about 15 dozen cookies

CHERRY THUMBPRINT COOKIES

¾ cup sugar
½ cup HELLMANN'S® or BEST
    FOODS® Real Mayonnaise
½ cup MAZOLA® Margarine
2 eggs, separated
1 teaspoon vanilla

2 cups all-purpose flour
¼ teaspoon ground nutmeg
1½ cups finely chopped
    walnuts or almonds
Red and green candied
    cherries

In large bowl, beat sugar, mayonnaise, margarine, egg yolks and vanilla. Beat in flour and nutmeg until well blended. Cover; refrigerate until firm, at least 3 hours.

Preheat oven to 350°F. Shape dough into ¾-inch balls. In small bowl, beat egg whites with fork until foamy. Dip each ball into egg whites; roll in nuts. Place, 1½ inches apart, on greased cookie sheets. Press thumb into centers of balls. Place one whole cherry in each center. Bake 15 to 17 minutes or until bottoms are browned. Let cookies cool slightly before removing them from cookie sheets to wire racks.

Makes about 5 dozen cookies

LEMON PECAN CRESCENTS

1 package DUNCAN HINES®
  Golden Sugar Cookie Mix
2 eggs
¾ cup toasted pecans,
  chopped

⅓ cup CRISCO® Oil or
  CRISCO® PURITAN®
  Canola Oil
¼ cup all-purpose flour
1 tablespoon grated lemon
  peel
Confectioners sugar

1. Preheat oven to 375°F.

2. Combine cookie mix, eggs, pecans, oil, flour and lemon peel in large bowl. Stir until thoroughly blended. Form level ½ measuring tablespoonfuls dough into crescent shapes. Place 2 inches apart on ungreased baking sheets. Bake at 375°F for 7 to 8 minutes or until set but not browned. Cool 2 minutes on baking sheets. Remove to cooling racks. Roll warm cookies in confectioners sugar. Cool completely. Roll cookies again in confectioners sugar. Store between layers of waxed paper in airtight container.

Makes about 6 dozen cookies

DATE-NUT MACAROONS

1 (8-ounce) package pitted
  dates, chopped
1½ cups flaked coconut
1 cup PLANTERS® Pecan
  Halves, chopped

¾ cup sweetened condensed
  milk (not evaporated
  milk)
½ teaspoon vanilla extract

Preheat oven to 350°F. In medium bowl, combine dates, coconut and nuts; blend in sweetened condensed milk and vanilla. Drop by rounded tablespoonfuls onto greased and floured cookie sheets. Bake for 10 to 12 minutes or until light golden brown. Carefully remove from cookie sheets; cool completely on wire racks. Store in airtight container.

Makes about 2 dozen cookies

Cookie Exchange Favorites

CHERRY RUM COOKIES

4 cups KELLOGGS'®
  SPECIAL K® cereal,
  crushed to 1½ cups,
  divided
2¼ cups all-purpose flour
 1 teaspoon baking powder
 ¼ teaspoon salt (optional)

½ cup margarine, softened
⅔ cup sugar
 1 egg
 1 teaspoon rum flavoring
10 to 12 maraschino cherries,
  cut into quarters

1. Stir together 1 cup of the crushed Kelloggs'® Special K® cereal, flour, baking powder and salt. Set aside.

2. In large mixing bowl, beat margarine and sugar until light and fluffy. Add egg and rum flavoring. Beat well. Add dry ingredients. Mix well.

3. Shape dough into balls using rounded measuring teaspoon. Roll in remaining ½ cup crushed cereal. Place on ungreased baking sheets. Top each cookie with cherry quarter.

4. Bake at 375°F about 12 minutes or until lightly browned. Remove immediately from baking sheets. Cool on wire racks. Store in airtight container. *Makes 3½ dozen*

Top to bottom: Corn Flake Macaroons (page 25),
Cherry Rum Cookies

CHOCOLATE-DIPPED BRANDY SNAPS

½ cup butter
½ cup sugar
⅓ cup dark corn syrup
½ teaspoon cinnamon
¼ teaspoon ginger
1 cup all-purpose flour
2 teaspoons brandy

1 cup (6-ounce package)
NESTLÉ® Toll House®
Semi-Sweet Chocolate
Morsels
1 tablespoon vegetable
shortening
⅓ cup finely chopped nuts

Preheat oven to 300°F. In heavy saucepan, combine butter, sugar, dark corn syrup, cinnamon and ginger; cook over medium heat, stirring constantly, until melted and smooth. Remove from heat; stir in flour and brandy. Drop mixture by rounded teaspoonfuls, about 3 inches apart, onto ungreased cookie sheets. (Do not bake more than 6 cookies at one time.)

Bake at 300°F for 10 to 12 minutes. Let stand a few seconds. Remove from cookie sheets and immediately roll around wooden spoon handle; cool completely. Combine over hot (not boiling) water, semi-sweet chocolate morsels and vegetable shortening; stir until morsels are melted and mixture is smooth. Dip each Brandy Snap halfway into melted chocolate. Sprinkle with nuts; set on waxed paper-lined cookie sheets. Chill until set. Store in airtight container in refrigerator.

Makes about 3 dozen (2½-inch) snaps

Chocolate-Dipped Brandy Snaps

CORN FLAKE MACAROONS

4 egg whites
1 teaspoon vanilla
¼ teaspoon cream of tartar
1⅓ cups sugar

1 cup chopped pecans
1 cup shredded coconut
3 cups KELLOGGS'® CORN
    FLAKES® cereal

1. Preheat oven to 325°F. In large mixing bowl, beat egg whites until foamy. Stir in vanilla and cream of tartar. Gradually add sugar, beating until stiff and glossy. Fold in pecans, coconut and Kellogg's® Corn Flakes® cereal. Drop mixture by rounded measuring tablespoons onto cookie sheets sprayed with vegetable cooking spray.

2. Bake about 15 minutes or until lightly browned. Remove immediately from cookie sheets. Cool on wire racks.   *Makes about 3 dozen cookies*

Variation: Fold in ½ cup crushed peppermint candy with pecans and coconut.

SANTA'S CHOCOLATE COOKIES

1 cup margarine or butter
⅔ cup semisweet chocolate
    chips
¾ cup sugar
1 egg
½ teaspoon vanilla

2 cups all-purpose flour
Apricot jam, melted
    semisweet chocolate,
    chopped almonds,
    frosting, coconut or
    colored sprinkles

Preheat oven to 350°F. Melt margarine with ⅔ cup chocolate chips in small saucepan over low heat, stirring until completely melted. Combine chocolate mixture and sugar in large bowl. Add egg and vanilla; stir well. Add flour; stir well. Refrigerate, covered, 30 minutes or until firm.

Shape dough into 1-inch balls or 2-inch logs. Place 1 inch apart on ungreased cookie sheets. If desired, flatten balls with bottom of drinking glass or make a depression in center and fill with jam.

Bake 8 to 10 minutes or until set. Remove to wire racks; cool completely. Decorate as desired with melted chocolate, almonds, frosting, coconut and colored sprinkles.   *Makes about 3 dozen cookies*

NO-BAKE PEANUTTY COOKIES

2 cups Roasted Honey Nut
SKIPPY® Creamy or
SUPER CHUNK® Peanut
Butter
2 cups graham cracker
crumbs
1 cup confectioners' sugar

½ cup KARO® Light or Dark
Corn Syrup
¼ cup semisweet chocolate
chips, melted
Colored sprinkles
(optional)

In large bowl, combine peanut butter, graham cracker crumbs,
confectioners' sugar and corn syrup. Mix until smooth. Shape into 1-inch
balls. Place on waxed paper-lined cookie sheets. Drizzle melted chocolate
over balls or roll in colored sprinkles. Store covered in refrigerator.

Makes about 5 dozen cookies

MELTING MOMENTS

1 cup flour
½ cup ARGO® or
KINGSFORD'S® Corn
Starch

½ cup confectioners sugar
¾ cup MAZOLA® Margarine,
softened
1 teaspoon vanilla

In medium bowl, combine flour, corn starch and confectioners sugar. In
large bowl with mixer at medium speed, beat margarine until smooth.
Add flour mixture and vanilla; beat until well blended. If necessary,
refrigerate dough 1 hour or until easy to handle.

Preheat oven to 350°F. Shape dough into 1-inch balls. Place, 1½ inches
apart, on ungreased cookie sheets; flatten with lightly floured fork. Bake
10 to 12 minutes or until edges are lightly browned. Remove from cookie
sheets; cool completely on wire racks. Store in tightly covered container.

Makes about 3 dozen cookies

Almond Melting Moments: Add 1 cup finely chopped almonds to flour
mixture.

Food Processor Method: In bowl of food processor with metal blade,
combine flour, corn starch and confectioners sugar. Cut cold margarine
into 1-inch pieces. Add to flour mixture. Process, adding vanilla through
feed tube, 15 seconds or until mixture forms a ball. Continue as above.

CHOCOLATE CHIP & MINT MERINGUE COOKIES

3 egg whites
½ teaspoon cream of tartar
  Pinch of salt
¾ cup sugar
4 drops green food coloring

4 drops mint extract
1 (6-ounce) package
  miniature semisweet
  chocolate chips

Preheat oven to 375°F. Grease and lightly flour two cookie sheets. Beat egg whites with cream of tartar and salt until foamy. Gradually beat in sugar, 2 tablespoons at a time, until soft peaks form. Stir in food coloring and mint extract. Fold in chocolate chips. Drop meringue by teaspoonfuls, 1 inch apart, onto prepared cookie sheets. Place in preheated oven. Turn off heat; let meringues set in oven 8 to 12 hours.

Makes about 4 dozen cookies

Chocolate Chip & Mint Meringue Cookies

CHOCO-CHERRY COOKIES SUPREME

2/3 cup all-purpose flour
1/2 cup unsweetened cocoa
1 1/2 teaspoons baking powder
1/2 teaspoon salt
1/3 cup butter or margarine, softened
1/2 cup granulated sugar
1/2 cup packed light brown sugar
1/3 cup milk

1 large egg
1 teaspoon vanilla
2 cups uncooked quick-cooking or old-fashioned oats
3 ounces white baking bar *or* white chocolate candy bar, cut into 1/4-inch pieces
1/2 cup candied cherries

Preheat oven to 375°F. Combine flour, cocoa, baking powder and salt; set aside. Beat butter and sugars in large bowl with electric mixer at medium speed until light and fluffy. Beat in milk, egg and vanilla, scraping down side of bowl once. Gradually add flour mixture. Stir in oats until well blended. Stir in baking bar pieces and cherries. Drop heaping teaspoonfuls of dough, 2 inches apart, onto greased cookie sheets. Bake 10 minutes or until set. Let stand on cookie sheets 1 minute. Remove cookies to wire racks; cool completely.   *Makes about 3 dozen cookies*

PECAN DROPS

3/4 cup sugar
1/2 cup FLEISCHMANN'S® Margarine, softened
1/4 cup EGG BEATERS® Real Egg Product
1 teaspoon vanilla extract

2 cups all-purpose flour
2/3 cup PLANTERS® Pecans, finely chopped
3 tablespoons jam, jelly or preserves, any flavor

In small bowl, with electric mixer at medium speed, cream sugar and margarine. Add Egg Beaters® and vanilla; beat for 1 minute. Stir in flour until blended. Chill dough for 1 hour.

Preheat oven to 350°F. Form dough into 36 (1 1/4-inch) balls; roll in pecans, pressing into dough. Place, 2 inches apart, on greased cookie sheets. Indent center of each ball with thumb or back of wooden spoon. Bake for 10 minutes; remove from oven. Spoon 1/4 teaspoon jam into each cookie indentation. Bake for 2 to 5 more minutes or until lightly browned. Remove from sheets; cool on wire racks.

Makes about 3 dozen cookies

Choco-Cherry Cookies Supreme

DATE MENENAS

2¾ cups all-purpose flour
½ teaspoon DAVIS® Baking
    Powder
¾ cup sugar, divided
⅔ cup FLEISCHMANN'S®
    Margarine, softened
1 teaspoon vanilla extract

¼ cup EGG BEATERS® Real
    Egg Product
8 ounces pitted dates, finely
    chopped
½ cup water
1 tablespoon lemon juice

In medium bowl, combine flour and baking powder. Set aside. Reserve 2 tablespoons sugar for date filling. In large bowl of electric mixer, on medium speed, beat margarine and remaining sugar until creamy. On low speed, add vanilla and Egg Beaters® alternately with flour mixture. Beat until well combined. Form into flattened disk; wrap in plastic wrap. Refrigerate 1 hour.

To make date filling, place dates, water, reserved sugar and lemon juice in medium saucepan. Bring to a boil. Reduce heat; simmer, covered, 10 minutes. Remove from heat; let cool to room temperature.

Preheat oven to 400°F. Cut dough in half. On floured waxed paper, roll each half of dough to 12×10-inch rectangle. Spread half the filling (½ cup) onto each dough piece. From long side, roll up as a jelly roll. With thread, cut log into ⅜-inch slices. Place on greased cookie sheets. Repeat with remaining dough and filling.

Bake at 10 minutes or until bottoms are lightly browned. Remove to wire rack to cool. Store in airtight container.

Makes about 5 dozen cookies

CHOCOLATE CHERRY CONFECTIONS

FUDGE FILLING
1½ cups semi-sweet chocolate
    chips
¾ cup sweetened condensed
    milk

3 tablespoons maraschino
    cherry juice

COOKIES
1 package DUNCAN HINES®
    Chocolate Chip Cookie
    Mix
1 egg
⅓ cup CRISCO® Oil or
    CRISCO® PURITAN®
    Canola Oil

⅓ cup chopped maraschino
    cherries, well drained
54 maraschino cherry halves,
    well drained, for garnish

Chocolate Cherry Confections

1. Preheat oven to 350°F.

2. **For Fudge Filling,** combine chocolate chips, sweetened condensed milk and maraschino cherry juice in small saucepan. Heat on low heat until chocolate chips are melted, stirring until smooth. Set aside.

3. **For Cookies,** combine cookie mix, egg and oil in large bowl. Stir until thoroughly blended. Stir in chopped maraschino cherries. Drop dough by rounded teaspoonfuls 2 inches apart onto ungreased baking sheets. Bake at 350°F for 5 minutes. Remove from oven. Drop 1 rounded teaspoonful fudge filling onto top of each partially baked cookie. Top each with maraschino cherry half. Bake 4 to 5 minutes longer or until edges are light golden brown. Cool 2 minutes on baking sheets. Remove to cooling racks. Cool completely. Store between layers of waxed paper in airtight container.   *Makes about 4 dozen cookies*

Chocolate Peanut Butter Cup Cookies

CHOCOLATE PEANUT BUTTER CUP COOKIES

COOKIES
- 1 cup semi-sweet chocolate chips
- 2 squares (1 ounce each) unsweetened baking chocolate
- 1 cup sugar
- ½ BUTTER FLAVOR* CRISCO® Stick or ½ cup BUTTER FLAVOR CRISCO all-vegetable shortening

DRIZZLE
- 1 cup peanut butter chips

- 2 eggs
- 1 teaspoon salt
- 1 teaspoon vanilla
- 1½ cups plus 2 tablespoons all-purpose flour
- ½ teaspoon baking soda
- ¾ cup finely chopped peanuts
- 36 miniature peanut butter cups, unwrapped

1. Heat oven to 350°F.

2. **For Cookies,** combine chocolate chips and chocolate squares in microwave-safe measuring cup or bowl. Microwave at 50% (MEDIUM) 2 minutes; stir. Repeat until smooth (or melt on rangetop in small saucepan on very low heat). Cool slightly.

3. Combine sugar and shortening in large bowl. Beat at medium speed of electric mixer until blended and crumbly. Beat in eggs, one at a time, then salt and vanilla. Reduce speed to low. Add chocolate slowly. Mix until well blended. Stir in flour and baking soda with spoon until well blended. Shape dough into 1¼-inch balls. Roll in nuts. Place, 2 inches apart, on ungreased cookie sheet.

4. Bake at 350°F for 8 to 10 minutes or until set. Immediately press peanut butter cup into center of each cookie. Press sides of cookie up against cup. Cool 2 minutes on cookie sheet before removing to cooling rack. Cool completely.

5. **For Drizzle,** place peanut butter chips in heavy resealable sandwich bag. Seal. Microwave at 50% (MEDIUM) 1 minute. Knead bag. Repeat until smooth (or melt by placing bag in hot water). Cut tiny tip off bottom corner of bag. Squeeze out and drizzle over cookies.

Makes about 3 dozen cookies

*Butter Flavor Crisco is artificially flavored.

TOFFEE TASSIES

½ cup margarine or butter
1 (3-ounce) package cream cheese, softened
1 cup all-purpose flour
¼ cup ground pecans
¾ cup packed brown sugar

1 egg
1 tablespoon margarine or butter, melted
½ cup chopped pecans
½ cup HEATH® Bits

For pastry, in a mixing bowl beat ½ cup margarine or butter and cream cheese until thoroughly combined. Stir in flour and ground pecans. Press a rounded teaspoon of pastry evenly into the bottom and up sides of 24 ungreased 1¾-inch miniature muffin cups. Set aside.

For filling, beat together brown sugar, egg and 1 tablespoon melted margarine or butter. Stir in chopped pecans. Spoon 1 teaspoon filling into each pastry-lined cup. Sprinkle about 1 teaspoon Heath® Bits over each. Bake in a 325°F oven about 30 minutes or until pastry is golden and filling is puffed. Cool slightly in pans on wire racks. Remove and cool completely on wire racks.

Makes 24 tassies

CHERRY COCONUT COOKIES

¾ cup sugar
¾ BUTTER FLAVOR* CRISCO®
 Stick or ¾ cup BUTTER
 FLAVOR CRISCO all-
 vegetable shortening
1 egg
1 teaspoon grated lemon
 peel
¾ teaspoon almond extract

½ teaspoon salt
1¾ cups all-purpose flour
1 teaspoon baking powder
½ teaspoon baking soda
¾ cup flaked coconut
½ cup coarsely chopped
 pecans
⅓ cup quartered maraschino
 cherries, well drained on
 paper towel

1. Preheat oven to 350°F.

2. Combine sugar, shortening, egg, lemon peel, almond extract and salt in large bowl. Beat at medium speed of electric mixer until well blended.

3. Combine flour, baking powder and baking soda. Add gradually to creamed mixture, mixing at low speed until blended. Stir in coconut, nuts and cherries with spoon. Shape dough into 1-inch balls. Place, 2 inches apart, on ungreased cookie sheet. Bake at 350°F for 11 to 12 minutes. Cool on cookie sheet 1 minute before removing to cooling rack.

Makes about 3½ dozen cookies

*Butter Flavor Crisco is artificially flavored.

CREAM CHEESE COOKIES

½ BUTTER FLAVOR* CRISCO®
 Stick or ½ cup BUTTER
 FLAVOR CRISCO all-
 vegetable shortening
1 package (3 ounces) cream
 cheese, softened

1 tablespoon milk
1 cup sugar
½ teaspoon vanilla
1 cup all-purpose flour
½ cup chopped pecans

1. Preheat oven to 375°F.

2. Combine shortening, cream cheese and milk in medium bowl. Beat at medium speed of electric mixer until well blended. Beat in sugar and vanilla. Mix in flour. Add nuts. Drop dough by level measuring tablespoonfuls, 2 inches apart, onto ungreased cookie sheet. Bake at 375°F for 10 minutes. Remove to cooling rack.

Makes about 3 dozen cookies

*Butter Flavor Crisco is artificially flavored.

Top to bottom: Cherry Coconut Cookies, Cream Cheese Cookies, Chocolate Thumbprints (page 36)

CHOCOLATE THUMBPRINTS

COOKIES

½ BUTTER FLAVOR* CRISCO® Stick or ½ cup BUTTER FLAVOR CRISCO all-vegetable shortening

½ cup granulated sugar

1 tablespoon milk

½ teaspoon vanilla

1 egg yolk

1 square (1 ounce) unsweetened baking chocolate, melted and cooled

1 cup all-purpose flour

¼ teaspoon salt

⅓ cup mini semisweet chocolate chips

PEANUT BUTTER CREAM FILLING

2 tablespoons BUTTER FLAVOR CRISCO® all-vegetable shortening

⅓ cup JIF® Creamy Peanut Butter

1 cup confectioners sugar

2 tablespoons milk

½ teaspoon vanilla

1. Preheat oven to 350°F. Grease cookie sheet with shortening.

2. **For Cookies,** combine ½ cup shortening, granulated sugar, milk, vanilla and egg yolk in large bowl. Beat at medium speed of electric mixer until well blended. Add melted chocolate. Mix well.

3. Combine flour and salt. Add gradually to chocolate mixture while mixing at low speed until blended. Add chocolate chips. Shape dough into 1-inch balls. Place, 2 inches apart, on greased cookie sheet. Press thumb gently into center of each cookie.

4. Bake at 350°F for 8 minutes. Press centers again with small measuring spoon. Remove to cooling rack. Cool completely.

5. **For Peanut Butter Cream Filling,** combine 2 tablespoons shortening and peanut butter in bowl. Stir until blended. Stir in confectioners sugar. Stir in 2 tablespoons milk and vanilla until smooth. Spoon into centers of cookies.   *Makes about 2½ dozen cookies*

*Butter Flavor Crisco is artificially flavored.

WALNUT JAM CRESCENTS

⅔ cup butter or margarine

1⅓ cups all-purpose flour

½ cup dairy sour cream

⅔ cup raspberry jam or orange marmalade

⅔ cup DIAMOND® Walnuts, finely chopped, divided

Preheat oven to 350°F. In medium bowl, cut butter into flour until mixture resembles fine crumbs. Add sour cream; mix until stiff dough is formed. Divide dough in half. Shape each half into a ball; flatten slightly. Wrap balls in waxed paper; chill well. Working with one half of dough at a time, roll dough into 11-inch round on lightly floured pastry cloth or board. Spread with 1/3 cup jam; sprinkle with 1/3 cup walnuts. Cut into quarters; cut each quarter into three wedges. Roll up, one at a time, starting from outer edge; place on lightly greased cookie sheets. Repeat with remaining half of dough and jam and nuts. Bake 25 to 30 minutes or until lightly browned. Remove to wire racks to cool.

Makes about 2 dozen crescents

AUSTRIAN TEA COOKIES

1½ cups sugar, divided
½ cup butter, softened
½ cup shortening
1 egg, beaten
½ teaspoon vanilla extract
2 cups all-purpose flour
2 cups ALMOND DELIGHT®
   Brand Cereal, crushed to
   1 cup

½ teaspoon baking powder
¼ teaspoon ground
   cinnamon
14 ounces almond paste
2 egg whites
5 tablespoons raspberry or
   apricot jam, warmed

In large bowl, beat 1 cup sugar, butter and shortening. Add egg and vanilla; mix well. Stir in flour, cereal, baking powder and cinnamon until well blended. Refrigerate 1 to 2 hours or until firm.

Preheat oven to 350°F. Roll dough out on lightly floured surface to ¼-inch thickness; cut into 2-inch circles with floured cookie cutter. Place on ungreased cookie sheet; set aside.

In small bowl, beat almond paste, egg whites and remaining ½ cup sugar until smooth. With pastry tube fitted with medium-sized star tip, pipe almond paste mixture, ½ inch thick, along outside edge of top of each cookie. Spoon about ¼ teaspoon jam into center of each cookie.

Bake 8 to 10 minutes or until lightly browned. Let stand 1 minute before removing from cookie sheet. Cool on wire rack.

Makes about 3½ dozen cookies

No-Bake Cherry Crisps

NO-BAKE CHERRY CRISPS

¼ cup butter or margarine,
    softened
1 cup powdered sugar
1 cup peanut butter
1⅓ cups crisp rice cereal
¼ cup plus 2 tablespoons
    mini semisweet
    chocolate chips

¼ cup chopped pecans
½ cup maraschino cherries,
    drained, dried and
    chopped
1 to 2 cups flaked coconut
    (for rolling)

In large mixing bowl, cream butter, sugar and peanut butter. Stir in cereal, chips, pecans and cherries. Mix well. Shape teaspoonfuls of dough into 1-inch balls. Roll in coconut. Put on cookie sheet; chill in refrigerator 1 hour. Store refrigerated. *Makes about 3 dozen treats*

CHOCOLATE ALMOND SNOWBALLS

1¾ cups all-purpose flour
⅔ cup NESTLÉ® Toll House®
   Baking Cocoa
2 teaspoons baking powder
¼ teaspoon salt
¾ cup granulated sugar

½ cup (1 stick) butter, melted
   and cooled
2 eggs
1 teaspoon almond extract
Confectioners' sugar

Preheat oven to 350°F. In small bowl, combine flour, cocoa, baking powder and salt; set aside.

In large mixer bowl, beat granulated sugar, butter, eggs and almond extract until creamy. Gradually add flour mixture, beating until well blended. Roll measuring tablespoonfuls of dough into balls. Place on ungreased cookie sheet.

Bake 6 to 8 minutes. Cool completely on wire racks. Sprinkle with confectioners' sugar.
Makes about 2½ dozen cookies

ORANGE DROP COOKIES

COOKIES

1 package DUNCAN HINES®
   Golden Sugar Cookie Mix
2 eggs
⅓ cup CRISCO® Oil or
   CRISCO® PURITAN®
   Canola Oil

1 tablespoon orange juice
½ teaspoon grated orange
   peel
¾ cup flaked coconut
½ cup chopped pecans

GLAZE

1½ cups confectioners sugar
1 tablespoon lemon juice
1 tablespoon orange juice

1½ teaspoons grated orange
   peel

1. Preheat oven to 375°F.

2. **For Cookies,** combine cookie mix, eggs, oil, 1 tablespoon orange juice and ½ teaspoon orange peel in bowl. Stir until well blended. Stir in coconut and pecans. Drop by rounded teaspoonfuls 2 inches apart onto ungreased baking sheets. Bake at 375°F for 7 to 8 minutes or until set. Cool 1 minute, then remove to cooling racks. Cool completely.

3. **For Glaze,** combine confectioners sugar, lemon juice, 1 tablespoon orange juice and 1½ teaspoons orange peel in small bowl. Stir until blended. Drizzle over tops of cooled cookies. Allow glaze to set before storing between layers of waxed paper in airtight container.
Makes about 4 dozen cookies

Creative Cutouts

FROSTED BUTTER COOKIES

COOKIES

1½ cups butter, softened
¾ cup granulated sugar
3 egg yolks
3 cups all-purpose flour

1 teaspoon baking powder
2 tablespoons orange juice
1 teaspoon vanilla

FROSTING

4 cups powdered sugar
½ cup butter, softened
3 to 4 tablespoons milk
2 teaspoons vanilla

Food coloring (optional)
Colored sugars, flaked
   coconut and cinnamon
   candies for decoration

For Cookies, in large bowl, cream butter and granulated sugar. Add yolks; beat until light and fluffy. Add flour, baking powder, orange juice and vanilla; beat until well mixed. Cover; refrigerate until firm, 2 to 3 hours.

Preheat oven to 350°F. Roll out dough, one half at a time, to ¼-inch thickness on well-floured surface. Cut out with holiday cookie cutters. Place, 1 inch apart, on ungreased cookie sheets. Bake 6 to 10 minutes or until edges are golden brown. Remove to wire racks to cool completely.

For Frosting, in medium bowl, combine all frosting ingredients except food coloring and decorations; beat until fluffy. If desired, divide frosting into small bowls; tint with food coloring. Frost cookies and decorate with colored sugars, coconut and candies.   *Makes about 3 dozen cookies*

Cinnamon Stars

CINNAMON STARS

2 tablespoons sugar
¾ teaspoon ground
    cinnamon
¾ cup butter or margarine,
    softened

2 egg yolks
1 teaspoon vanilla extract
1 package DUNCAN HINES®
    Moist Deluxe French
    Vanilla Cake Mix

1. Preheat oven to 375°F.

2. Combine sugar and cinnamon in small bowl. Set aside.

3. Combine butter, egg yolks and vanilla extract in large bowl. Blend in cake mix gradually. Roll to ⅛-inch thickness on lightly floured surface. Cut with 2½-inch star cookie cutter. Place, 2 inches apart, on ungreased cookie sheets. Sprinkle cookies with cinnamon-sugar mixture. Bake at 375°F for 6 to 8 minutes or until edges are light golden brown. Cool 1 minute on cookie sheets. Remove to cooling racks. Cool completely. Store in airtight container. *Makes 3 to 3½ dozen cookies*

COCOA ALMOND CUT-OUT COOKIES

¾ cup margarine or butter,
   softened
1 (14-ounce) can EAGLE®
   Brand Sweetened
   Condensed Milk (NOT
   evaporated milk)
2 eggs
1 teaspoon vanilla extract

½ teaspoon almond extract
2¾ cups unsifted flour
⅔ cup HERSHEY'S Cocoa
2 teaspoons baking powder
½ teaspoon baking soda
½ cup finely chopped
   almonds
Chocolate Glaze

In large mixer bowl, beat margarine, sweetened condensed milk, eggs and extracts until well blended. Combine dry ingredients; add to margarine mixture, beating until well blended. Stir in almonds. Divide dough into four equal portions. Wrap each in plastic wrap; flatten. Chill until firm enough to roll, about 2 hours.

Preheat oven to 350°F. Working with one portion at a time (keep remaining dough in refrigerator), on floured surface, roll to about ⅛-inch thickness. Cut into desired shapes. Place on lightly greased baking sheets. Bake 6 to 8 minutes or until set. Remove from baking sheets. Cool completely. Drizzle with Chocolate Glaze. Store tightly covered at room temperature.

Makes about 6 dozen (3-inch) cookies

Chocolate Glaze: Melt 1 cup (6 ounces) HERSHEY'S Semi-Sweet Chocolate Chips with 2 tablespoon shortening. Makes about ⅔ cup.

HOLIDAY GINGERBREAD PEOPLE

1 (14½-ounce) package
   gingerbread mix
⅓ cup orange juice
1 tablespoon grated orange
   rind
½ teaspoon ground
   cinnamon

1 cup confectioners' sugar
4 teaspoons milk
½ cup "M&M's®" Plain
   Chocolate Candies

Preheat oven to 375°F. In mixing bowl, blend gingerbread mix, orange juice, rind and cinnamon until smooth. Turn dough onto floured surface; knead until smooth. Form into a ball; divide in half. Roll out half of dough to ⅛-inch thickness. With a 6-inch cookie cutter, cut three or four cookie people, carefully placing on lightly greased baking sheet. Re-roll dough scraps; cut to make eight cookies in all. Repeat with remaining half of dough. Bake 6 to 8 minutes or until firm. Cool slightly; remove to wire rack to cool completely. Combine confectioners' sugar and milk; mix until well blended. Spoon into icing bag fitted with writing tip. Outline cookies with frosting. Decorate with candies. *Makes 16 cookies*

Kittens and Mittens

KITTENS AND MITTENS

1 recipe Chocolate Cookie
   dough (see next page)
1 recipe Cookie Glaze
   (see next page)

Assorted candies

1. Preheat oven to 325°F. Grease cookie sheets.

2. Roll dough on floured surface to ⅛-inch thickness. Using diagrams
1 and 2 on next page as guides, cut out kitten and mitten cookies. Place
cookies on prepared cookie sheets. With plastic straw, make holes in tops
of cookies, about ½ inch from top edges.

3. Bake 8 to 10 minutes until edges begin to brown. Remove to wire
racks; cool completely. If necessary, push straw through warm cookies to
remake holes.

4. Place cookies on racks on waxed paper-lined baking sheets. Spoon
glaze over cookies. Place some of remaining glaze in small plastic food
storage bag. Cut tiny tip from corner of bag. Use to pipe decorations as
shown in photo. Decorate with candies as shown. Let stand until glaze
has set.

5. Thread yarn or ribbon through holes to make garland.

Makes about 2 dozen cookies

CHOCOLATE COOKIES

1 cup butter or margarine,
   softened
1 cup sugar
1 egg
1 teaspoon vanilla

2 ounces semisweet
   chocolate, melted
2¼ cups all-purpose flour
1 teaspoon baking powder
¼ teaspoon salt

1. Beat butter and sugar in large bowl at high speed of electric mixer until fluffy. Beat in egg and vanilla. Add melted chocolate; mix well. Add flour, baking powder and salt; mix well. Cover; refrigerate until firm, about 2 hours.

2. Preheat oven to 325°F. Grease cookie sheets. Roll dough on floured surface to ⅛-inch thickness. Cut into desired shapes with cookie cutters. Place on prepared cookie sheets.

3. Bake 8 to 10 minutes or until set. Remove to wire racks; cool completely.   *Makes about 3 dozen cookies*

COOKIE GLAZE

4 cups confectioners' sugar
4 to 6 tablespoons milk

Assorted food colors

1. Combine confectioners' sugar and enough milk to make a medium-thick pourable glaze. Spoon Cookie Glaze into several small bowls. Color as desired with food colors.

2. Place cookies on wire rack on waxed paper-lined baking sheet. Spoon glaze over cookies; allow to dry completely.

Makes about 4 cups glaze

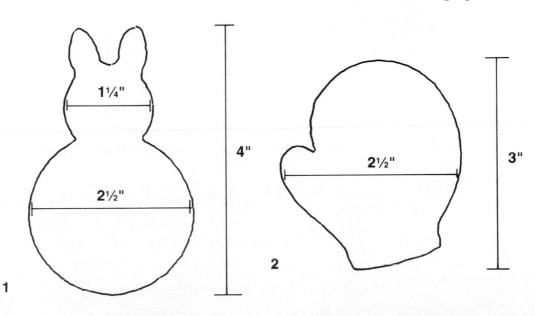

HANUKKAH COOKIES

COOKIES

¾ cup butter or margarine, softened

2 egg yolks

2 tablespoons grated orange peel

1 package DUNCAN HINES® Moist Deluxe White Cake Mix

FROSTING

1 container (16 ounces) DUNCAN HINES® Creamy Homestyle Vanilla Frosting

3 to 4 drops blue food coloring

3 to 4 drops yellow food coloring

1. **For Cookies,** combine butter, egg yolks and orange peel in large bowl. Beat at low speed with electric mixer until blended. Add cake mix gradually, beating until thoroughly blended. Form dough into ball. Cover with plastic wrap and refrigerate for 1 to 2 hours or until chilled but not firm.

2. Preheat oven to 375°F.

3. Roll dough to ⅛-inch thickness on lightly floured surface. Cut with Hanukkah cookie cutters. Place, 2 inches apart, on ungreased cookie sheets. Bake at 375°F for 6 to 7 minutes or until edges are light golden brown. Cool 1 minute on cookie sheets. Remove to cooling racks. Cool completely.

4. **For Frosting,** tint ½ cup vanilla frosting with blue food coloring. Warm frosting in microwave oven at HIGH (100% power) for 5 to 10 seconds, if desired. Place writing tip in pastry bag. Fill with tinted frosting. Pipe outline pattern on cookies (see photo). Tint ½ cup frosting with yellow food coloring and leave ½ cup frosting untinted; decorate as desired. Allow frosting to set before storing cookies between layers of waxed paper in airtight container.   *Makes 3½ to 4 dozen cookies*

CHRISTMAS STAINED GLASS COOKIES

Hard candies (in assorted
   colors)
¾ cup butter, softened
¾ cup white granulated sugar
2 eggs

1 teaspoon vanilla extract
3 cups all-purpose flour
1 teaspoon baking powder
Frosting (optional)
Candy (optional)

Separate colors of hard candy. Place each color of candy in small freezer-weight plastic food storage bag; crush with a wooden mallet.* In a mixing bowl, beat together butter and sugar. Beat in eggs and vanilla. Combine flour and baking powder. Gradually stir into butter mixture until dough is very stiff. Wrap in plastic wrap; chill about 3 hours.

Preheat oven to 375°F. Roll out dough to ⅛-inch thickness on lightly floured surface. Additional flour can be added, if necessary. Cut out cookies using large Christmas cookie cutters. Transfer cookies to a foil-lined baking sheet. Using a small Christmas cookie cutter of the same shape as the large one, cut out and remove dough from center of each cookie.** Fill cut-out sections with crushed candy. If using cookies as hanging ornaments, make holes with a chopstick at top of cookies for string. Bake 7 to 9 minutes or until cookies are lightly browned and candy is melted. Slide foil off baking sheets. When cool, carefully loosen cookies from foil. If desired, decorate with frosting and other candies.

Makes about 2½ dozen medium cookies

*You will need a total measurement of about ⅓ cup crushed.

**Other shapes can be used to cut out center to make different designs.

Favorite recipe from **The Sugar Association, Inc.**

CHOCOLATE GINGERBREAD COOKIES

COOKIES
2¼ cups all-purpose flour
¾ cup NESTLÉ® Toll House®
   Baking Cocoa
1 teaspoon baking soda
1 teaspoon ginger
½ teaspoon baking powder
½ teaspoon cinnamon

½ teaspoon cloves
¼ teaspoon salt
½ cup (1 stick) butter or
   margarine, softened
1 cup granulated sugar
1 egg
½ cup molasses

GLAZE
1 cup confectioners' sugar
2 to 3 tablespoons milk

1 foil-wrapped bar
   (2 ounces) NESTLÉ®
   Semi-Sweet Chocolate
   Baking Bar, broken up

Cookies: In small bowl, combine flour, cocoa, baking soda, ginger, baking powder, cinnamon, cloves and salt; set aside.

In large mixer bowl, beat butter and granulated sugar until creamy. Blend in egg and molasses. Gradually beat in flour mixture. Divide dough into four equal pieces; wrap in plastic wrap. Refrigerate at least 2 hours until firm.

Preheat oven to 350°F. Lightly grease two large cookie sheets. On floured board, roll dough, one piece at a time, to ⅛-inch thickness. Cut with 4½-inch cookie cutters. With metal spatula, transfer cutouts to prepared cookie sheets. Repeat with remaining dough.

Bake 8 to 10 minutes until set. Let stand 2 minutes. Remove from cookie sheets; cool completely.

Glaze: In small bowl, combine confectioners' sugar and 2 tablespoons milk; stir until smooth. (Add additional 1 tablespoon milk if necessary for desired consistency.) Set aside.

In small saucepan over low heat, melt baking bar. Pipe cookies with Glaze or decorate with melted semi-sweet chocolate baking bar.

Makes about 2 dozen cookies

Chocolate Gingerbread Cookies

ORANGE-SPICED GINGERBREAD CUTOUTS

1¼ cups butter or margarine,
    softened, divided
½ cup firmly packed brown
    sugar
⅔ cup light molasses
1 egg
1½ teaspoons grated lemon
    peel
2½ cups all-purpose flour
1¼ teaspoons ground
    cinnamon

3 teaspoons vanilla, divided
1 teaspoon ground allspice
½ teaspoon baking soda
½ teaspoon salt
½ teaspoon ground ginger
¼ teaspoon baking powder
4 cups powdered sugar
4 tablespoons milk
    Food coloring (optional)

Beat ¾ cup butter, brown sugar, molasses, egg and lemon peel in large bowl with electric mixer until smooth. Add flour, cinnamon, 1 teaspoon vanilla, allspice, baking soda, salt, ginger and baking powder. Beat until well mixed. Shape dough into a disk and wrap in plastic wrap. Refrigerate at least 2 hours.

Preheat oven to 350°F. Grease cookie sheets; set aside. Roll out half of dough on floured surface with floured rolling pin to ¼-inch thickness. Cut out with 3- to 4-inch cookie cutters. Place 1 inch apart on prepared cookie sheets. Bake 6 to 8 minutes or until set. Remove cookies to wire rack; cool completely.

Beat powdered sugar, remaining ½ cup butter, milk and 2 teaspoons vanilla in medium bowl with electric mixer until fluffy. Tint frosting with food coloring, if desired. Decorate cooled cookies with frosting.

Makes about 4 dozen cookies

Orange-Spiced Gingerbread Cutouts,
Santa's Chocolate Cookies (page 25)

VERSATILE CUT-OUT COOKIES

3½ cups unsifted flour
1 tablespoon baking powder
½ teaspoon salt
1 (14-ounce) can EAGLE®
    Brand Sweetened
    Condensed Milk (NOT
    evaporated milk)

¾ cup margarine or butter,
    softened
2 eggs
1 tablespoon vanilla extract
    or 2 teaspoons almond or
    lemon extract

Combine flour, baking powder and salt. In large mixer bowl, beat sweetened condensed milk, margarine, eggs and vanilla until well blended. Add dry ingredients; mix well. Cover; chill 2 hours.

Preheat oven to 350°F. On floured surface, knead dough to form a smooth ball. Divide into thirds. On well-floured surface, roll out each portion to ⅛-inch thickness. Cut with floured cookie cutter. Reroll as necessary to use all dough. Place, 1 inch apart, on greased cookie sheets. Bake 7 to 9 minutes or until lightly browned around edges (do not overbake). Cool. Frost and decorate as desired. Store loosely covered at room temperature.

Makes about 6½ dozen cookies

Chocolate Cookies: Decrease flour to 3 cups. Add ½ cup HERSHEY®S Cocoa to dry ingredients. Chill and roll dough as directed. Makes about 6½ dozen cookies.

Versatile Cut-Out Cookies

Sandwich Cookies: Prepare, chill and roll dough as directed. Use 2½-inch floured cookie cutter. Bake as directed. Sandwich two cookies together with ready-to-spread frosting. Sprinkle tops with confectioners' sugar, if desired. Makes about 3 dozen cookies.

Cookie Pecan Critters: Prepare and chill dough as directed. For each critter, arrange three pecan halves together on ungreased cookie sheets. Shape 1 teaspoonful dough into 1-inch ball. Press firmly onto center of arranged pecans. Repeat until all dough is used. Bake 12 to 14 minutes. Spread tops with Chocolate Frosting.* Makes about 6½ dozen cookies.

***Chocolate Frosting:** In small saucepan, melt ¼ cup margarine or butter with ¼ cup water. Stir in ½ cup HERSHEY'S Cocoa. Remove saucepan from heat; beat in 2 cups confectioners' sugar and 1 teaspoon vanilla until smooth. Stir in additional water for a thinner consistency, if desired. Makes about 1 cup.

Mincemeat Peek-a-Boo Cookies: Prepare, chill and roll dough as directed. Use 3-inch floured round cookie cutter. Using sharp knife, cut "X" in center of half the rounds. Place 1 teaspoon mincemeat in center of remaining rounds. Top with cut rounds. Bake 8 to 10 minutes. Cool. Sprinkle with confectioners' sugar, if desired. Makes about 4 dozen cookies.

Stained Glass Cookies: Prepare, chill and roll dough as directed. Use 3-inch floured cookie cutter to cut into desired shapes. Cut out holes for "stained glass" in each cookie with small cutters or knife. Place on aluminum foil-lined cookie sheets. Fill holes with crushed hard candies. (If planning to hang cookies, make hole in each cookie in dough near edge with straw.) Bake 6 to 8 minutes or until candy has melted. Cool 10 minutes; remove from foil. Makes about 8 dozen cookies.

Cinnamon Pinwheel Cookies: Decrease baking powder to 2 teaspoons. Prepare and chill dough as directed. Divide into quarters. Roll each quarter of dough into a 16 × 8-inch rectangle. Brush with melted margarine or butter. Top each with 2 tablespoons sugar combined with ½ teaspoon ground cinnamon. Roll up tightly, beginning at 8-inch side. Wrap tightly; freeze until firm, about 20 minutes. Unwrap; cut into ¼-inch slices. Place on ungreased cookie sheets. Bake 12 to 14 minutes or until lightly browned. Makes about 6½ dozen cookies.

Chocolate Snow Balls: Prepare dough as directed for Chocolate Cookies, increasing eggs to three; add 1 cup finely chopped nuts. Chill. Shape into 1-inch balls. Roll in confectioners' sugar. Bake 8 to 10 minutes. Cool. Roll again in confectioners' sugar. Makes about 7½ dozen cookies.

GINGERBREAD COOKIES

½ cup shortening
⅓ cup packed light brown
  sugar
¼ cup dark molasses
1 egg white
½ teaspoon vanilla
1½ cups all-purpose flour

½ teaspoon baking soda
½ teaspoon salt
¼ teaspoon baking powder
1 teaspoon ground
  cinnamon
½ teaspoon ground ginger

1. Beat shortening, brown sugar, molasses, egg white and vanilla in large bowl at high speed of electric mixer until smooth. Combine flour, baking soda, salt, baking powder and spices in small bowl. Add to shortening mixture; mix well. Cover; refrigerate until firm, about 8 hours or overnight.

2. Preheat oven to 350°F. Grease cookie sheets.

3. Roll dough on floured surface to ⅛-inch thickness. Cut into desired shapes with cookie cutters. Place on prepared cookie sheets.

4. Bake 6 to 8 minutes or until edges begin to brown. Remove to wire racks; cool completely.   *Makes about 2½ dozen cookies*

BLACK AND WHITE CUT-OUTS

2¾ cups *plus* 2 tablespoons
  all-purpose flour, divided
1 teaspoon baking soda
¾ teaspoon salt
1 cup butter or margarine,
  softened
¾ cup granulated sugar
¾ cup packed light brown
  sugar
2 large eggs

1 teaspoon vanilla
¼ cup unsweetened cocoa
4 ounces white baking bar,
  broken into ½-inch
  pieces
4 ounces semisweet
  chocolate chips
Assorted decorative
  candies (optional)

Combine 2¾ cups flour, baking soda and salt in medium bowl; mix well. Beat butter and sugars in large bowl until light and fluffy. Beat in eggs, one at a time. Beat in vanilla. Gradually add flour mixture. Beat until well blended. Remove half of dough from bowl; reserve. To make chocolate dough, beat cocoa into remaining dough with spoon until well blended. To make butter cookie dough, beat remaining 2 tablespoons flour into reserved dough. Flatten each piece of dough into a disc; wrap in plastic wrap and refrigerate about 1½ hours or until firm. (Dough may be refrigerated up to 3 days before baking.)

Black and White Cut-Outs

Preheat oven to 375°F. Working with one type of dough at a time, place dough on lightly floured surface. Roll out dough to ¼-inch thickness. Cut dough into desired shapes with cookie cutters. Place cut-outs, 1 inch apart, on cookie sheets. Bake 9 to 11 minutes or until set. Let cookies stand on cookie sheets 2 minutes. Remove cookies to wire rack; cool completely.

For white chocolate drizzle, place baking bar pieces in small resealable plastic freezer bag; seal bag. Heat in microwave oven at MEDIUM (50% power) 2 minutes. Turn bag over; heat at MEDIUM (50% power) 2 to 3 minutes or until melted. Knead bag until baking bar is completely smooth. Cut very tiny corner off bottom of bag; pipe or drizzle baking bar onto chocolate cookies. Decorate as desired with assorted candies. Let stand until white chocolate is set, about 30 minutes.

For chocolate drizzle, place chocolate chips in small resealable plastic freezer bag; seal bag. Heat in microwave oven at HIGH 1 minute. Turn bag over; heat at HIGH 1 to 2 minutes or until chocolate is melted. Knead bag until chocolate is completely smooth. Cut tiny corner off bottom of bag; pipe or drizzle chocolate onto butter cookies. Decorate as desired with assorted candies. Let stand until chocolate is set, about 40 minutes.

Makes 3 to 4 dozen cookies

Black and White Sandwiches: Cut cookies out with same cookie cutter. Spread thin layer of prepared frosting onto bottom side of chocolate cookie. Place bottom side of butter cookie over frosting. Drizzle either side of cookie with melted chocolate or white chocolate.

PEEK-A-BOO APRICOT COOKIES

4 ounces bittersweet
  chocolate candy bar,
  broken into pieces
3 cups all-purpose flour
½ teaspoon baking soda
½ teaspoon salt

⅔ cup butter or margarine,
  softened
¾ cup sugar
2 large eggs
2 teaspoons vanilla
Apricot preserves

Melt chocolate in small bowl set in bowl of very hot water, stirring twice. Set aside to cool. Combine flour, baking soda and salt in medium bowl; mix well. Set aside. Beat butter and sugar in large bowl until light and fluffy. Beat in eggs, one at a time, scraping down side of bowl after each addition. Beat in vanilla and chocolate. Gradually add flour mixture. Divide dough into two rounds; wrap in plastic wrap. Refrigerate 2 hours or until firm.

Preheat oven to 350°F. Roll out dough on lightly floured surface to ¼- to ⅛-inch thickness. Cut out dough with 2½-inch round cutter. Cut 1-inch centers out of half of circles. Remove scraps of dough from around and within circles; reserve. Place on ungreased cookie sheets. Repeat rolling and cutting with remaining scraps of dough. Bake cookies 9 to 10 minutes or until set. Let cookies stand on cookie sheets 2 minutes. Remove cookies to wire racks; cool completely. To assemble cookies, spread about 1½ teaspoons preserves over each cookie circle; close with cut-out cookies to form a sandwich.   *Makes about 1½ dozen cookies*

LINZER HEARTS

1 package DUNCAN HINES®
  Golden Sugar Cookie Mix
½ cup finely ground almonds
1 egg
¼ cup CRISCO® Oil or
  CRISCO® PURITAN®
  Canola Oil

1½ tablespoons water
  Confectioners sugar
⅔ cup seedless red raspberry
  jam, warmed

1. Preheat oven to 375°F.

2. Combine cookie mix, almonds, egg, oil and water in large bowl. Stir with spoon until blended. Roll dough ⅛ inch thick on lightly floured board. Cut out 3-inch hearts with floured cookie cutter. Cut out centers of half the hearts with smaller heart cookie cutter. Reroll dough as needed. Place 2 inches apart on ungreased baking sheets. Bake whole hearts at 375°F for 8 to 9 minutes and cut-out hearts for 6 to 7 minutes or until edges are lightly browned. Cool 1 minute on baking sheets. Remove to cooling racks. Cool completely.

3. To assemble, dust cut-out hearts with sifted confectioners sugar. Spread warm jam over whole hearts almost to edge. Top with cut-out hearts. Fill center with ¼ teaspoon jam.   *Makes 30 (3-inch) sandwich cookies*

Tip: If you like a softer cookie, make these a day ahead.

YULE TREE NAMESAKES

1 recipe Gingerbread Cookie dough (page 54)	**Assorted candies**
1 recipe Cookie Glaze (page 45)	**3 packages (12 ounces each) semisweet chocolate chips, melted**
Green food color	**1 cup flaked coconut, tinted green***
Confectioners' sugar	

1. Preheat oven to 350°F. Roll dough on floured surface to ⅛-inch thickness. Cut out cookies using tree-shaped cookie cutter. Place, 2 inches apart, on ungreased cookie sheets.

2. Bake 12 to 14 minutes until edges begin to brown. Remove to wire racks; cool completely.

3. Reserve ⅓ cup Cookie Glaze; color remaining glaze green with food color. Place cookies on wire rack over waxed paper-lined baking sheet. Spoon green glaze over cookies.

4. Add 1 to 2 tablespoons confectioners' sugar to reserved Cookie Glaze. Spoon into pastry bag fitted with small writing tip. Pipe names onto trees. Decorate with assorted candies. Let stand until glaze is set.

5. Spoon melted chocolate into baking cups or tartlet pans, filling evenly. Let stand until chocolate is very thick and partially set. Place trees, standing upright, in chocolate.

6. Sprinkle tinted coconut over chocolate.   *Makes 24 place cards*

***Tinting coconut:** Dilute a few drops of food color with ½ teaspoon water in a large plastic food storage bag. Add 1 to 1⅓ cups flaked coconut. Close bag and shake well until the coconut is evenly coated. If a deeper color is desired, add more diluted food color and shake again.

Cookie Jar Classics

SPICY PUMPKIN COOKIES

2 CRISCO® Sticks or 2 cups
  CRISCO all-vegetable
  shortening
2 cups sugar
1 can (16 ounces) pumpkin
2 eggs
2 teaspoons vanilla
4 cups all-purpose flour
2 teaspoons baking powder

2 teaspoons ground
  cinnamon
1 teaspoon salt
1 teaspoon baking soda
1 teaspoon ground nutmeg
½ teaspoon ground allspice
2 cups raisins
1 cup chopped nuts

1. Preheat oven to 350°F.

2. Combine shortening, sugar, pumpkin, eggs and vanilla in large bowl; beat well.

3. Combine flour, baking powder, cinnamon, salt, baking soda, nutmeg and allspice. Add to batter; mix well. Stir in raisins and nuts. Drop rounded teaspoonfuls of dough, 2 inches apart, onto greased cookie sheet.

4. Bake at 350°F for 12 to 15 minutes. Cool on rack. If desired, frost with vanilla frosting.   *Makes about 7 dozen cookies*

Top to bottom: Drop Sugar Cookies (page 61),
Spicy Pumpkin Cookies

Top to bottom: Chocolate Orange Granola Cookies,
Double Chocolate Cookies

DOUBLE CHOCOLATE COOKIES

2¼ cups all-purpose flour
1 teaspoon baking soda
1 teaspoon salt
1 cup butter, softened
¾ cup granulated sugar
¾ cup firmly packed brown sugar
1 teaspoon vanilla extract
2 eggs

Two envelopes (2 ounces) NESTLÉ® Choco-Bake® Unsweetened Baking Chocolate Flavor
One 12-ounce package (2 cups) NESTLÉ® Toll House® Semi-Sweet Chocolate Morsels
1 cup chopped walnuts

Preheat oven to 375°F. In medium bowl, combine flour, baking soda and salt; set aside. In large bowl, combine butter, granulated sugar, brown sugar and vanilla extract; beat until creamy. Beat in eggs and unsweetened baking chocolate flavor. Gradually beat in flour mixture. Stir in morsels and nuts. Drop by rounded teaspoonfuls onto ungreased cookie sheets. Bake at 375°F for 8 to 10 minutes. Cool completely on wire racks.   *Makes about 6 dozen (2½-inch) cookies*

CHOCOLATE ORANGE GRANOLA COOKIES

1 cup all-purpose flour
½ teaspoon baking powder
½ teaspoon allspice
½ teaspoon salt
⅔ cup firmly packed brown
   sugar
½ cup butter, softened
1 egg
1 teaspoon vanilla extract

½ teaspoon grated orange
   rind
1¼ cups granola cereal
One 6-ounce package
   (1 cup) NESTLÉ® Toll
   House® Semi-Sweet
   Chocolate Morsels
½ cup flaked coconut
¼ cup chopped nuts

Preheat oven to 350°F. In small bowl, combine flour, baking powder, allspice and salt; set aside. In large bowl, combine brown sugar and butter; beat until creamy. Add egg, vanilla extract and orange rind; beat well. Gradually beat in flour mixture. Stir in granola cereal, morsels, coconut and nuts. Drop by rounded tablespoonfuls onto ungreased cookie sheets. Sprinkle with additional coconut, if desired. Bake at 350°F for 9 to 11 minutes. Cool completely on wire racks.

Makes about 1½ dozen (2-inch) cookies

DROP SUGAR COOKIES

⅓ cup CRISCO® Oil
1 cup sugar
1 tablespoon vanilla
1 egg

2½ cups all-purpose flour
¾ teaspoon salt
½ teaspoon baking soda
¼ cup skim milk

1. Preheat oven to 400°F. Oil cookie sheet lightly.

2. Combine ⅓ cup Crisco® Oil, sugar and vanilla in large bowl. Add egg. Beat at medium speed of electric mixer until blended. Stir in flour, salt and baking soda with spoon. Stir until mixture is smooth. Add milk. Stir until well blended.

3. Drop dough by teaspoonfuls, 2 inches apart, onto cookie sheet. Flatten cookies with bottom of glass lightly oiled and dipped in sugar (or colored sugar).

4. Bake at 400°F for 6 to 8 minutes or until barely browned around edges. *Do not overbake.* Remove to cooling rack.

Makes about 3 dozen cookies

SOFT SPICY MOLASSES COOKIES

2 cups all-purpose flour
1 cup sugar
3/4 cup butter, softened
1/3 cup light molasses
3 tablespoons milk
1 egg
1/2 teaspoon baking soda
1/2 teaspoon ground ginger
1/2 teaspoon ground
  cinnamon
1/2 teaspoon ground cloves
1/8 teaspoon salt
Sugar for rolling

In large mixer bowl, combine flour, 1 cup sugar, butter, molasses, milk, egg, baking soda, ginger, cinnamon, cloves and salt. Beat at low speed, scraping bowl often, until well mixed, 2 to 3 minutes. Cover; refrigerate until firm, at least 4 hours or overnight.

Preheat oven to 350°F. Shape rounded teaspoonfuls of dough into 1-inch balls. Roll in sugar. Place, 2 inches apart, on ungreased cookie sheets. Bake 10 to 12 minutes or until slightly firm to the touch. Remove immediately.   *Makes about 4 dozen cookies*

BUTTER-FLAVORED BRICKLE DRIZZLES

COOKIES

1 BUTTER FLAVOR* CRISCO®
  Stick or 1 cup BUTTER
  FLAVOR CRISCO all-
  vegetable shortening
1 cup granulated sugar
1 cup firmly packed brown
  sugar

1 can (14 ounces) sweetened
  condensed milk (not
  evaporated milk)
1 teaspoon vanilla
1 3/4 cups all-purpose flour
1 teaspoon salt
1/2 teaspoon baking soda
3 cups quick oats, uncooked
1 cup almond brickle chips

DRIZZLE
1 cup milk chocolate chips

1. Preheat oven to 350°F. Grease cookie sheet with shortening.

2. **For Cookies,** combine 1 cup shortening, granulated sugar and brown sugar in large bowl. Stir with spoon until well blended and creamy. Stir in condensed milk and vanilla. Mix well.

3. Combine flour, salt and baking soda. Stir into creamed mixture. Stir in oats.

4. Shape dough into 1-inch balls. Press tops into brickle chips. Place, brickle side up, 2 inches apart on greased cookie sheet. Bake at 350°F for 9 to 10 minutes or until set but not browned. Remove to cooling rack. Cool completely.

5. **For Drizzle,** place chocolate chips in heavy resealable sandwich bag. Seal. Microwave at 50% (MEDIUM). Knead bag after 1 minute. Repeat until smooth (or melt by placing in bowl of hot water). Cut tiny tip off bottom corner of bag. Squeeze out and drizzle over cookies.

Makes about 6 dozen cookies

*Butter Flavor Crisco is artificially flavored.

Butter-Flavored Brickle Drizzles

ALMOND MILK CHOCOLATE CHIPPERS

1¼ cups all-purpose flour
½ teaspoon baking soda
½ teaspoon salt
½ cup butter or margarine, softened
½ cup packed light brown sugar

⅓ cup granulated sugar
1 large egg
2 tablespoons almond-flavored liqueur
1 cup milk chocolate chips
½ cup slivered almonds, toasted

Preheat oven to 375°F. Combine dry ingredients; mix until well blended. Set aside. Beat butter, brown sugar and granulated sugar in large bowl until light and fluffy. Beat in egg until well blended. Beat in liqueur. Gradually add dry ingredients. Beat until well blended. Stir in chips and almonds. Drop dough by rounded teaspoonfuls, 2 inches apart, onto ungreased cookie sheets. Bake 9 to 10 minutes or until edges arc golden brown. Let cookies stand on cookies sheets 2 minutes. Remove cookies with spatula to wire racks; cool completely.

Makes about 3 dozen cookies

RAISIN SPICE DROPS

¾ cup (1½ sticks) margarine, softened
⅔ cup firmly packed brown sugar
⅔ cup granulated sugar
2 eggs
1 teaspoon vanilla
2½ cups QUAKER® Oats (quick or old fashioned, uncooked)

1¼ cups all-purpose flour
1 teaspoon cinnamon
½ teaspoon baking soda
½ teaspoon salt (optional)
¼ teaspoon nutmeg
⅔ cup raisins
½ cup chopped nuts

Preheat oven to 350°F. Beat margarine and sugars until fluffy. Blend in eggs and vanilla. Add remaining ingredients; mix well. Drop dough by rounded teaspoonfuls onto ungreased cookie sheet. Bake 8 to 10 minutes or until light golden brown. Cool on wire rack. Store tightly covered.

Makes about 4½ dozen cookies

Almond Milk Chocolate Chippers

PINEAPPLE CARROT COOKIES

2 cans (8 ounces *each*)
 DOLE® Crushed
 Pineapple in Juice
¾ cup margarine, softened
½ cup brown sugar, packed
½ cup granulated sugar
1 egg
1 teaspoon vanilla extract
1 cup shredded DOLE®
 Carrots

1 cup chopped walnuts
1 cup DOLE® Raisins
1½ cups all-purpose flour
1 teaspoon ground
 cinnamon
½ teaspoon ground ginger
½ teaspoon baking powder
¼ teaspoon salt

Preheat oven to 375°F.

Drain pineapple well, reserving juice for beverage or another use.

Beat margarine and sugars until light and fluffy. Beat in egg and vanilla. Beat in pineapple, carrots, nuts and raisins.

Combine remaining ingredients; beat into pineapple mixture until well blended.

Drop dough by heaping tablespoonfuls onto greased cookie sheets. Flatten tops with spoon. Bake 15 to 20 minutes.

Makes about 3 dozen cookies

Prep Time: 20 minutes
Bake Time: 20 minutes per batch

OATMEAL MACAROONS

1 cup (2 sticks) margarine or
 butter, softened
1 cup firmly packed brown
 sugar
2 eggs
½ teaspoon almond extract
1¼ cups all-purpose flour

1 teaspoon baking soda
3 cups QUAKER® Oats (quick
 or old fashioned),
 uncooked
1⅓ cups (4-ounce package)
 flaked or shredded
 coconut

Preheat oven to 350°F. Lightly grease cookie sheet. Beat margarine and sugar until fluffy. Blend in eggs and almond extract. Add combined flour and baking soda; mix well. Stir in oats and coconut. Drop dough by rounded teaspoonfuls onto prepared cookie sheet. Bake 10 minutes or until light golden brown. Cool 2 minutes on cookie sheet; remove to wire rack. Cool completely. Store tightly covered.

Makes about 4½ dozen cookies

Choco-Scutterbotch

CHOCO-SCUTTERBOTCH

²/₃ **BUTTER FLAVOR* CRISCO®**
  Stick or ²/₃ cup BUTTER
  FLAVOR CRISCO all-
  vegetable shortening
¹/₂ **cup firmly packed brown**
  sugar
 2 eggs
 1 package DUNCAN HINES®
  Moist Deluxe Yellow
  Cake Mix

 1 cup toasted rice cereal
¹/₂ **cup milk chocolate chunks**
¹/₂ **cup butterscotch chips**
¹/₂ **cup semi-sweet chocolate**
  chips
¹/₂ **cup coarsely chopped**
  walnuts or pecans

1. Preheat oven to 375°F. Combine shortening and brown sugar in large bowl. Beat at medium speed of electric mixer until well blended. Beat in eggs.

2. Add cake mix gradually at low speed. Mix until well blended. Stir in cereal, chocolate chunks, butterscotch chips, chocolate chips and nuts with spoon until well blended. Shape dough into 1¼-inch balls. Place, 2 inches apart, on ungreased cookie sheet. Flatten slightly. Shape sides to form circle, if necessary.

3. Bake at 375°F for 7 to 9 minutes or until lightly browned around edges. Cool 2 minutes before removing to paper towels to cool completely.

Makes about 3 dozen cookies

*Butter Flavor Crisco is artificially flavored.

PEANUT BUTTER SENSATIONS

1 cup JIF® Creamy Peanut
  Butter
¾ cup granulated sugar
½ cup firmly packed brown
  sugar
½ BUTTER FLAVOR* CRISCO®
  Stick or ½ cup BUTTER
  FLAVOR CRISCO all-
  vegetable shortening

1 tablespoon milk
1 teaspoon vanilla
1 egg
1¼ cups all-purpose flour
¾ teaspoon baking soda
½ teaspoon baking powder
¼ teaspoon salt

1. Preheat oven to 375°F. Combine peanut butter, granulated sugar, brown sugar, shortening, milk and vanilla in large bowl. Beat at medium speed of electric mixer until well blended. Beat in egg.

2. Combine flour, baking soda, baking powder and salt. Add gradually to creamed mixture at low speed. Mix just until blended. Drop by rounded tablespoonfuls, 2 inches apart, onto ungreased cookie sheet. Make crisscross marks on top of dough with floured fork tines. Bake at 375°F for 8 to 10 minutes. Cool 2 minutes on cookie sheet before removing to cooling rack.   *Makes about 2 dozen cookies*

*Butter Flavor Crisco is artificially flavored.

***Clockwise from top: Old-Fashioned Oatmeal Cookies (page 70),
Peanut Butter Sensations, Ultimate Chocolate Chip Cookies***

ULTIMATE CHOCOLATE CHIP COOKIES

¾ BUTTER FLAVOR* CRISCO®
Stick or ¾ cup BUTTER
FLAVOR CRISCO all-
vegetable shortening
1¼ cups firmly packed brown
sugar
2 tablespoons milk
1 tablespoon vanilla

1 egg
1¾ cups all-purpose flour
1 teaspoon salt
¾ teaspoon baking soda
1 cup semi-sweet chocolate
chips
1 cup coarsely chopped
pecans**

1. Preheat oven to 375°F.

2. Combine shortening, sugar, milk and vanilla in large bowl. Beat at medium speed of electric mixer until well blended. Beat in egg.

3. Combine flour, salt and baking soda. Mix into creamed mixture at low speed until just blended. Stir in chocolate chips and nuts.

4. Drop rounded tablespoonfuls of dough, 3 inches apart, onto ungreased cookie sheet.

5. Bake at 375°F for 8 to 10 minutes for chewy cookies (they will look light and moist—do not overbake), 11 to 13 minutes for crisp cookies. Cool 2 minutes on cookie sheet. Remove to cooling rack.

Makes about 3 dozen cookies

*Butter Flavor Crisco is artificially flavored.

**You may substitute an additional ½ cup semi-sweet chocolate chips for the pecans.

Variations

Drizzle: Combine 1 teaspoon BUTTER FLAVOR CRISCO and 1 cup semi-sweet chocolate chips or 1 cup white melting chocolate, cut into small pieces, in microwave-safe measuring cup. Microwave at 50% (MEDIUM) 1 minute. Stir. Repeat until smooth (or melt on rangetop in small saucepan on very low heat). To thin, add a little more Butter Flavor Crisco. Drizzle back and forth over cookies. Sprinkle with nuts before chocolate hardens, if desired. To quickly harden chocolate, place cookies in refrigerator for a few minutes.

Chocolate Dipped: Melt chocolate as directed for Drizzle. Dip one end of each cooled cookie halfway into chocolate. Sprinkle with finely chopped nuts before chocolate hardens. Place on waxed paper until chocolate is firm. To quickly harden chocolate, place cookies in refrigerator for a few minutes.

OLD-FASHIONED OATMEAL COOKIES

¾ BUTTER FLAVOR* CRISCO®
   Stick or ¾ cup BUTTER
   FLAVOR CRISCO all-
   vegetable shortening
1¼ cups firmly packed brown
   sugar
 1 egg
⅓ cup milk
1½ teaspoons vanilla

1 cup all-purpose flour
½ teaspoon baking soda
½ teaspoon salt
¼ teaspoon cinnamon
3 cups quick oats (not instant
   or old fashioned)
1 cup raisins
1 cup coarsely chopped
   walnuts

1. Preheat oven to 375°F. Grease cookie sheet with Butter Flavor Crisco.

2. Combine ¾ cup shortening, sugar, egg, milk and vanilla in large bowl. Beat at medium speed of electric mixer until well blended. Combine flour, baking soda, salt and cinnamon. Mix into creamed mixture at low speed until just blended. Stir in oats, raisins and nuts with spoon.

3. Drop rounded tablespoonfuls of dough, 2 inches apart, onto prepared cookie sheet.

4. Bake at 375°F for 10 to 12 minutes or until lightly browned. Cool 2 minutes on cookie sheet. Remove to cooling rack.

Makes about 2½ dozen cookies

*Butter Flavor Crisco is artificially flavored.

PEANUT BUTTER REFRIGERATOR COOKIES

2½ cups flour
 1 teaspoon baking powder
 1 teaspoon baking soda
¼ teaspoon salt
 1 cup SKIPPY® Creamy or
   SUPER CHUNK® Peanut
   Butter

1 cup MAZOLA® Margarine
1 cup granulated sugar
1 cup packed brown sugar
2 eggs
1 teaspoon vanilla

In small bowl, combine flour, baking powder, baking soda and salt. In large bowl with mixer at medium speed, beat peanut butter and margarine until smooth. Beat in sugars until blended. Beat in eggs and vanilla. Add flour mixture; beat until well blended. Shape dough into two rolls, 1½ inches in diameter. Wrap in plastic wrap; refrigerate until firm.

Preheat oven to 350°F. Slice rolls into ¼-inch-thick slices. Place, 2 inches apart, on ungreased cookie sheets. Bake 12 minutes or until lightly browned. Remove; cool completely on wire racks. Store in tightly covered container.

Makes about 8 dozen cookies

APPLESAUCE OATMEAL COOKIES

1 cup all-purpose flour
1 teaspoon baking powder
1 teaspoon ground allspice
1 teaspoon cinnamon
½ teaspoon nutmeg
½ teaspoon cloves
¼ teaspoon salt

½ cup margarine
½ cup packed brown sugar
2 egg whites
2 cups rolled oats
1 cup unsweetened
　applesauce
½ cup chopped raisins

Preheat oven to 375°F. Grease baking sheet. Mix flour, baking powder, spices and salt. Beat margarine and sugar until creamy. Add egg whites; beat well. Add dry ingredients. Stir in oats, applesauce and raisins. Drop by level tablespoonfuls onto baking sheet. Bake 10 to 12 minutes or until edges are lightly browned. Cool on rack before serving.

Makes about 4 dozen cookies

Favorite recipe from **New York Apple Association, Inc.**

BUTTERSCOTCH FRUIT DROPS

2 cups all-purpose flour
1 teaspoon baking soda
½ teaspoon salt
½ cup (1 stick) butter or
　margarine, softened
¾ cup firmly packed brown
　sugar
1 egg
2 tablespoons milk

1 teaspoon grated lemon
　rind, optional
One 12-ounce package (2 cups)
　NESTLÉ® Toll House®
　Butterscotch Flavored
　Morsels
1 cup diced mixed dried fruit
　bits or raisins

Preheat oven to 350°F. In small bowl, combine flour, baking soda and salt; set aside.

In large mixer bowl, beat butter and brown sugar until creamy. Blend in egg, milk and lemon rind. Gradually beat in flour mixture. Stir in morsels and fruit. Drop by rounded measuring teaspoonfuls onto ungreased cookie sheets.

Bake 9 to 11 minutes until golden brown. Let stand 2 minutes. Remove from cookie sheets; cool on wire racks.   *Makes about 6 dozen cookies*

SNICKERDOODLES

3 tablespoons sugar
1 teaspoon ground
   cinnamon
1 package (18.25 ounces)
   DUNCAN HINES® Moist
   Deluxe Yellow Cake Mix

2 eggs
¼ cup CRISCO® Oil or
   CRISCO® PURITAN®
   Canola Oil

1. Preheat oven to 375°F. Grease cookie sheet.

2. Combine sugar and cinnamon in small bowl.

3. Combine cake mix, eggs and oil in large bowl. Stir until well blended. Shape dough into one-inch balls. Roll in cinnamon-sugar mixture. Place balls, 2 inches apart, on cookie sheet. Flatten balls with bottom of glass.

4. Bake at 375°F for 8 to 9 minutes or until set. Cool one minute on cookie sheet before removing to wire rack.

Makes about 3 dozen cookies

PECAN CRUNCHIES

1 package DUNCAN HINES®
   Golden Sugar Cookie Mix
2 eggs
⅓ cup CRISCO® Oil or
   CRISCO® PURITAN®
   Canola Oil

1 teaspoon water
2 cups crushed potato chips,
   divided
⅔ cup chopped pecans

1. Preheat oven to 375°F. Grease cookie sheets lightly.

2. Combine cookie mix, eggs, oil, water, ½ cup potato chips and pecans in large bowl. Stir until thoroughly blended. Form dough into 48 (1-inch) balls. Roll in remaining 1½ cups crushed potato chips. Place 2 inches apart on baking sheets. Flatten dough with fork.

3. Bake at 375°F for 8 to 10 minutes or until golden brown. Cool 1 minute on baking sheets. Remove to cooling racks. Cool completely. Store in airtight container.

Makes 4 dozen cookies

Top to bottom: Snickerdoodles, Pecan Crunchies

Banana Drop Cookies

BANANA DROP COOKIES

2 ripe, medium DOLE®
 Bananas
1 cup margarine, softened
1 cup granulated sugar
½ cup packed brown sugar
2 eggs
1 teaspoon vanilla
2 cups all-purpose flour

1 teaspoon baking soda
1 teaspoon ground
 cinnamon (optional)
½ teaspoon salt
1 cup peanut butter chips
1 cup chopped walnuts
1 cup raisins

Preheat oven to 375°F.

Cut bananas into chunks. In food processor or blender, process bananas
until smooth. In large bowl, cream margarine and sugars. Beat in
bananas, eggs and vanilla. In small bowl, combine flour, baking soda,
cinnamon and salt. Gradually beat flour mixture into banana mixture.
Stir in chips, nuts and raisins. Drop dough by tablespoonfuls, 2 inches
apart, onto greased cookie sheets. Bake 12 minutes or until golden
brown. Cool on wire racks.   *Makes about 4 dozen cookies*

ALMOND DELIGHTFUL COOKIES

¼ cup (½ stick) margarine or
  butter, softened
¼ cup vegetable shortening
½ cup packed brown sugar
¼ cup sugar
1 egg, beaten
1 teaspoon vanilla extract

1 cup all-purpose flour
1 teaspoon baking powder
3 cups ALMOND DELIGIIT®
  Brand Cercal, crushed to
  1½ cups
½ cup semi-sweet chocolate
  pieces *or* raisins

Preheat oven to 350°F. Lightly grease cookie sheet. In large bowl, cream margarine, shortening and sugars. Add egg and vanilla; mix well. Stir in flour and baking powder until well combined. Add cereal and chocolate pieces; mix well. Drop by level tablespoons onto prepared cookie sheet. Bake 10 to 12 minutes or until lightly browned. Let stand 1 minute before removing from cookie sheet. Cool on wire rack.

Makes about 2½ dozen cookies

CHOCO PEANUT BUTTER DREAMS

1½ cups firmly packed brown
  sugar
1 cup creamy or chunk-style
  peanut butter
¾ cup (1½ sticks) margarine
⅓ cup water
1 egg
1 teaspoon vanilla
3 cups QUAKER® Oats (quick
  or old fashioned,
  uncooked)

1½ cups all-purpose flour
½ teaspoon baking soda
1½ cups semi-sweet chocolate
  pieces
4 teaspoons vegetable
  shortening
⅓ cup chopped peanuts
  (optional)

Preheat oven to 350°F. Beat brown sugar, peanut butter and margarine until fluffy. Blend in water, egg and vanilla. Add combined oats, flour and baking soda; mix well. Shape into 1-inch balls. Place on ungreased cookie sheet. Using bottom of glass dipped in sugar, press into ¼-inch-thick circles. Bake 8 to 10 minutes or until edges are golden brown. Remove to wire rack; cool completely.

In saucepan over low heat, melt chocolate pieces and shortening, stirring until smooth.* Top each cookie with ½ teaspoon melted chocolate; sprinkle with chopped peanuts. Chill until set. Store tightly covered.

Makes about 6 dozen cookies

Microwave Directions: Place chocolate pieces and shortening in microwavable bowl. Microwave at HIGH 1 to 2 minutes, stirring after 1 minute and then every 30 seconds until smooth.

Brownie & Bar Bonanza

▲   ▲   ▲

APPLE CRUMB SQUARES

2 cups QUAKER® Oats (Quick or Old Fashioned), uncooked
1½ cups all-purpose flour
1 cup packed brown sugar
1 teaspoon ground cinnamon
½ teaspoon salt (optional)

½ teaspoon baking soda
¼ teaspoon ground nutmeg
¾ cup butter or margarine, melted
1 cup commercially prepared applesauce
½ cup chopped nuts

Preheat oven to 350°F. In large bowl, combine all ingredients except applesauce and nuts; mix until crumbly. Reserve 1 cup oats mixture. Press remaining oats mixture onto bottom of greased 13×9-inch pan. Bake 13 to 15 minutes; cool. Spread applesauce over partially baked crust; sprinkle with nuts. Sprinkle reserved 1 cup oats mixture over top. Bake 13 to 15 minutes or until golden brown. Cool in pan on wire rack; cut into 2-inch squares.   *Makes about 24 squares*

Apple Crumb Squares

FUDGY WALNUT COOKIE WEDGES

1 (20-ounce) package refrigerated cookie dough, any flavor
1 (12-ounce) package semisweet chocolate chips
2 tablespoons margarine or butter
1 (14-ounce) can EAGLE® Brand Sweetened Condensed Milk (NOT evaporated milk)
1 teaspoon vanilla extract
½ cup chopped walnuts

Preheat oven to 350°F. Divide cookie dough into thirds. With floured hands, press onto bottom of three aluminum foil-lined 9-inch round cake pans or press into 9-inch circles on ungreased baking sheets. Bake 10 to 20 minutes or until golden. Cool. In heavy saucepan, over medium heat, melt chips and margarine with sweetened condensed milk. Cook and stir until thickened, about 5 minutes; add vanilla. Spread over cookie circles. Top with walnuts. Chill. Cut into wedges. Store loosely covered at room temperature. *Makes about 36 wedges*

Fudgy Walnut Cookie Wedges

PUMPKIN JINGLE BARS

¾ cup MIRACLE WHIP® Salad
  Dressing
1 two-layer spice cake mix
1 (16-ounce) can pumpkin
3 eggs

Confectioners' sugar
Vanilla frosting
Red and green gum drops,
  sliced

Preheat oven to 350°F. Mix first 4 ingredients in large bowl at medium speed of electric mixer until well blended. Pour into greased 15½×10½-inch jelly roll pan. Bake 18 to 20 minutes or until edges pull away from sides of pan. Cool. Sprinkle with sugar. Cut into bars. Decorate with frosting and gum drops.   *Makes about 36 bars*

Preparation time: 5 minutes
Baking time: 20 minutes

LEMON CRUNCHIES

1 (14- or 15-ounce) can
  sweetened condensed
  milk
½ cup lemon juice
1 teaspoon grated lemon
  peel
2 to 3 drops yellow food
  coloring
1½ cups sifted all-purpose
  flour

1 teaspoon DAVIS® Baking
  Powder
1 teaspoon salt
⅔ cup margarine, softened
1 cup firmly packed light
  brown sugar
1 cup quick-cooking oats

Blend milk, juice, lemon peel and food coloring; set aside.

Sift together flour, baking powder and salt. With mixer, beat margarine and sugar until creamy; mix in flour mixture and oats until crumbly.

Pat half the oat mixture onto bottom of a well greased 8×8-inch pan. Spread milk mixture over crust; sprinkle with remaining oat mixture. Bake 30 minutes or until browned around pan edges. Cool in pan on wire rack for about 15 minutes; cut into bars. Chill until firm.

Makes about 24 bars

ULTIMATE DESIGNER BROWNIES

¾ cup HERSHEY'S Cocoa
½ teaspoon baking soda
⅔ cup butter or margarine,
   melted and divided
½ cup boiling water
2 cups sugar
2 eggs
1⅓ cups all-purpose flour
1 teaspoon vanilla extract
¼ teaspoon salt

¾ cup (3½-ounce jar)
   macadamia nuts,
   coarsely chopped
2 cups (12-ounce package)
   HERSHEY'S Semi-Sweet
   Chocolate Chips, divided
Vanilla Glaze (recipe
   follows)
½ teaspoon shortening (not
   butter, margarine or oil)

Preheat oven to 350°F. Grease 13×9-inch baking pan or two 8-inch square baking pans. In medium bowl, stir together cocoa and baking soda; blend in ⅓ cup melted butter. Add boiling water; stir until mixture thickens. Stir in sugar, eggs and remaining ⅓ cup melted butter; stir until smooth. Add flour, vanilla and salt; blend well. Stir in nuts and 1½ cups chocolate chips. Pour into prepared pan(s). Bake 30 to 35 minutes for square pans or 35 to 40 minutes for rectangular pan or until brownie begins to pull away from sides of pan. Cool completely in pan on wire rack.

Prepare Vanilla Glaze; spread Vanilla Glaze on top of brownies. Cut brownies into triangles. Place remaining ½ cup chips and shortening in top of double boiler over hot, not boiling, water; stir until melted. Put into pastry bag fitted with small writing tip. Pipe design on each brownie.

Makes about 24 brownies

VANILLA GLAZE

2 tablespoons butter or
   margarine
4 teaspoons milk

¼ teaspoon brandy extract
¼ teaspoon rum extract
1 cup powdered sugar

In small saucepan over low heat, melt butter in milk. Remove from heat; add brandy and rum extracts. Gradually add powdered sugar, beating with wire whisk until smooth. Makes about ½ cup glaze.

Streusel Caramel Bars

STREUSEL CARAMEL BARS

2 cups unsifted flour
¾ cup firmly packed light
    brown sugar
1 egg, beaten
¾ cup cold margarine or
    butter
¾ cup chopped nuts

24 EAGLE™ Brand Caramels,
    unwrapped
1 (14-ounce) can EAGLE®
    Brand Sweetened
    Condensed Milk (NOT
    evaporated milk)

Preheat oven to 350°F. In large bowl, combine flour, sugar and egg; cut in
½ cup margarine until crumbly. Stir in nuts. Reserving 2 cups crumb
mixture, press remainder firmly onto bottom of greased 13 × 9-inch
baking pan. Bake 15 minutes. Meanwhile, in heavy saucepan, over low
heat, melt caramels with sweetened condensed milk and remaining
¼ cup margarine. Pour over prepared crust. Top with reserved crumb
mixture. Bake 20 minutes or until bubbly. Cool. Cut into bars. Store
loosely covered at room temperature.   *Makes 24 to 36 bars*

Chocolate Caramel Bars: Melt 2 (1-ounce) squares unsweetened
chocolate with caramels, sweetened condensed milk and margarine.
Proceed as above.

CHOCOLATE CARAMEL-PECAN BARS

2 cups butter, softened,
   divided
½ cup granulated sugar
1 large egg
2¾ cups all-purpose flour
⅔ cup packed light brown
   sugar

¼ cup light corn syrup
2½ cups coarsely chopped
   pecans
1 cup semisweet chocolate
   chips

Preheat oven to 375°F. Grease 15×10-inch jelly-roll pan; set aside. Beat 1 cup butter and granulated sugar in large bowl until light and fluffy. Beat in egg. Add flour. Beat until well combined. Spread dough with rubber spatula into prepared pan. Bake 20 minutes or until light golden brown.

While bars are baking, prepare topping. Combine remaining 1 cup butter, brown sugar and corn syrup in medium, heavy saucepan. Cook over medium heat until mixture boils, stirring frequently. Boil gently 2 minutes, without stirring. Quickly stir in pecans; spread evenly over base. Return to oven. Bake 20 minutes or until dark golden brown and bubbling. Immediately sprinkle chocolate chips evenly over hot caramel. Gently press chips into caramel topping with spatula. Loosen caramel from edges of pan with a thin spatula or knife. Remove pan to wire rack; cool completely. Cut into 3×1½-inch bars.   *Makes about 40 bars*

BUTTERSCOTCH BROWNIES

2 cups all-purpose flour
2 teaspoons baking powder
1½ teaspoons salt
One 12-ounce package (2 cups)
   NESTLÉ® Toll House®
   Butterscotch Flavored
   Morsels

½ cup (1 stick) butter
1 cup firmly packed brown
   sugar
4 eggs
1 teaspoon vanilla extract
1 cup chopped nuts

Preheat oven to 350°F. In small bowl, combine flour, baking powder and salt; set aside. Combine over hot (not boiling) water, butterscotch flavored morsels and butter. Stir until morsels are melted and mixture is smooth. Transfer to large mixer bowl. Stir in brown sugar; cool 5 minutes. Beat in eggs and vanilla extract. Blend in flour mixture. Stir in nuts. Spread in greased 15½×10½-inch baking pan.

Bake 20 minutes. Cool. Cut into 2-inch squares.

Makes about 35 brownies

Chocolate Caramel-Pecan Bars

PINEAPPLE ALMOND SHORTBREAD BARS

CRUST
1½ cups all-purpose flour
½ cup DOLE® Almonds,
    toasted, ground

¼ cup sugar
½ cup cold margarine

TOPPING
1 can (20 ounces) DOLE®
    Crushed Pineapple,
    drained
3 eggs
¼ cup sugar

¼ cup honey
1 tablespoon grated lemon
    peel
1½ cups DOLE® Slivered
    Almonds, toasted

For Crust, preheat oven to 350°F. In large bowl, combine flour, ground almonds and sugar. Cut in margarine until crumbly. Form dough into a ball; press into ungreased 13×9-inch baking pan. Bake 10 minutes. Cool slightly.

For Topping, in medium bowl, combine pineapple, eggs, sugar, honey and lemon peel. Stir in toasted almonds. Pour topping over partially baked crust. Bake an additional 30 to 35 minutes. Cool completely in pan on wire rack. Cut into bars.   *Makes about 2 dozen bars*

APPLE MACADAMIA NUT BAR

3 Golden Delicious apples,
    chopped small
1 tablespoon lemon juice
1 (16-ounce) box pound cake
    mix
1 cup milk
1 teaspoon grated lemon
    peel

½ teaspoon almond extract
1 cup flaked, sweetened
    coconut
3½ ounces macadamia nuts,
    coarsely chopped
3½ ounces white chocolate,
    coarsely chopped

1. Heat oven to 350°F. Grease and flour 13×9-inch baking pan. Combine apples and lemon juice; set aside.

2. In large bowl, with electric mixer, beat together dry pound cake mix, milk, lemon peel and almond extract. Stir in coconut, macadamia nuts, white chocolate and the reserved apples; mix well.

3. Spoon batter into prepared pan. Bake 50 to 55 minutes or until center springs back when gently pressed. Cool in pan 5 minutes; cut into bars.
                                                        Makes 12 bars

---

Favorite recipe from **Washington Apple Commission**

MAGIC COOKIE BARS

½ cup margarine or butter
1½ cups graham cracker
    crumbs
1 (14-ounce) can EAGLE®
    Brand Sweetened
    Condensed Milk (NOT
    evaporated milk)

1 (6-ounce) package semi-
    sweet chocolate chips
1 (3½-ounce) can flaked
    coconut (1½ cups)
1 cup chopped nuts

Preheat oven to 350°F (325°F for glass dish). In 13×9-inch baking pan, melt margarine in oven. Sprinkle crumbs over margarine; pour sweetened condensed milk evenly over crumbs. Top with remaining ingredients; press down firmly. Bake 25 to 30 minutes or until lightly browned. Cool. Chill if desired. Cut into bars. Store loosely covered at room temperature. *Makes 24 to 36 bars*

Seven Layer Magic Cookie Bars: Add 1 (6-ounce) package butterscotch flavored chips after chocolate chips.

Magic Peanut Cookie Bars: Omit chocolate chips and chopped nuts. Top sweetened condensed milk with 2 cups (about ¾ pound) chocolate-covered peanuts, then coconut. Proceed as above.

Magic Cookie Bars

Cherry Chewbilees

CHERRY CHEWBILEES

CRUST
1 cup walnut pieces, divided
1¼ cups all-purpose flour
½ cup firmly packed brown
    sugar

½ cup BUTTER FLAVOR*
    CRISCO® Stick or ½ cup
    BUTTER FLAVOR CRISCO
    all-vegetable shortening
½ cup flaked coconut

FILLING
2 packages (8 ounces each)
    cream cheese, softened
⅔ cup granulated sugar
2 eggs

2 teaspoons vanilla
1 can (21 ounces) cherry pie
    filling

1. Preheat oven to 350°F. Grease 13×9-inch pan with shortening. Set aside. Chop ½ cup nuts coarsely for topping. Set aside. Chop remaining ½ cup nuts finely.

2. **For Crust,** combine flour and brown sugar. Cut in ½ cup shortening until fine crumbs form. Add ½ cup finely chopped nuts and coconut. Mix well. Remove ½ cup coconut mixture. Set aside. Press remaining coconut mixture onto bottom of pan. Bake at 350°F for 12 to 15 minutes, until edges are lightly browned.

3. **For Filling,** beat cream cheese, granulated sugar, eggs and vanilla in small bowl at medium speed of electric mixer until smooth. Spread over hot baked crust. Return to oven. Bake 15 minutes longer or until set. Spread cherry pie filling over cheese layer. Combine reserved coarsely chopped nuts and reserved coconut mixture. Sprinkle evenly over cherries. Return to oven. Bake 15 minutes longer. Chill. Refrigerate several hours. Cut into $2 \times 1\frac{1}{2}$-inch bars.   *Makes about 36 bars*

*Butter Flavor Crisco is artificially flavored.

GERMAN SWEET CHOCOLATE CREAM CHEESE BROWNIES

BROWNIE LAYER

1 package (4 ounces) BAKER'S® GERMAN'S® Sweet Chocolate

¼ cup (½ stick) margarine or butter

¾ cup sugar

2 eggs

1 teaspoon vanilla

½ cup all-purpose flour

½ cup chopped nuts

CREAM CHEESE LAYER

4 ounces PHILADELPHIA BRAND® Cream Cheese, softened

¼ cup sugar

1 egg

1 tablespoon all-purpose flour

Preheat oven to 350°F.

Microwave chocolate and margarine in large microwavable bowl on HIGH 2 minutes or until margarine is melted. Stir until chocolate is completely melted.

Stir ¾ cup sugar into melted chocolate mixture. Mix in 2 eggs and vanilla until well blended. Stir in ½ cup flour and nuts. Spread in greased 8-inch square pan.

Mix cream cheese, ¼ cup sugar, 1 egg and 1 tablespoon flour in same bowl until smooth. Place spoonfuls over brownie batter. Swirl with knife to marbleize.

Bake for 35 minutes or until toothpick inserted into center comes out with fudgy crumbs. Do not overbake. Cool in pan; cut into squares.

Makes about 16 brownies

Prep time: 20 minutes
Baking time: 35 minutes

CHOCOLATE SCOTCHEROOS

1 cup light corn syrup
1 cup sugar
1 cup peanut butter
6 cups KELLOGGS'® RICE
    KRISPIES® Cereal
Vegetable cooking spray

1 package (6 ounces, 1 cup)
    semi-sweet chocolate
    morsels
1 package (6 ounces, 1 cup)
    butterscotch morsels

1. Measure corn syrup and sugar into large saucepan. Cook over medium heat, stirring frequently, until sugar dissolves and mixture begins to boil. Remove from heat. Stir in peanut butter. Mix well. Add Kellogg's® Rice Krispies® Cereal. Stir until well coated. Press mixture into 13 × 9-inch pan coated with cooking spray. Set aside.

2. Melt chocolate and butterscotch morsels together in small saucepan over low heat, stirring constantly. Spread evenly over cereal mixture. Let stand until firm. Cut into 2 × 1-inch bars to serve.

Makes about 48 bars

CHOCOLATE CHUNK BLONDE BROWNIES

½ cup (1 stick) margarine or
    butter, softened
1 cup firmly packed brown
    sugar
1 cup granulated sugar
4 eggs
2 teaspoons vanilla
2 cups all-purpose flour

1 teaspoon CALUMET®
    Baking Powder
¼ teaspoon salt
1 package (8 ounces)
    BAKER'S® Semi-Sweet
    Chocolate, coarsely
    chopped
1 cup chopped nuts

Preheat oven to 350°F.

Beat margarine, sugars, eggs and vanilla until light and fluffy. Mix in flour, baking powder and salt until well blended. Stir in chocolate and nuts. Spread into greased 13 × 9-inch pan.

Bake for 30 minutes or until toothpick inserted into center comes out with moist crumbs. Do not overbake. Cool in pan; cut into squares.

Makes about 24 brownies

Prep time: 20 minutes
Baking time: 30 minutes

CRANBERRY JEWEL BARS

2 cups unsifted flour
1½ cups quick-cooking or
  old-fashioned oats
¾ cup plus 1 tablespoon
  firmly packed brown
  sugar
1 cup *cold* margarine or
  butter
1 (14-ounce) can EAGLE®
  Brand Sweetened
  Condensed Milk (NOT
  evaporated milk)

1 cup ricotta cheese
2 eggs
1½ teaspoons vanilla extract
1 teaspoon grated orange
  rind
2 tablespoons cornstarch
1 (16-ounce) can whole berry
  cranberry sauce

Preheat oven to 350°F. In large bowl, combine flour, oats and ¾ *cup* sugar. Cut in *cold* margarine until crumbly. Reserving 2 cups crumb mixture, press remainder firmly onto bottom of 13×9-inch baking pan. Bake 15 minutes.

Meanwhile, in small mixer bowl, beat sweetened condensed milk, cheese, eggs, vanilla and rind until smooth. Spread evenly over baked crust. In small bowl, combine remaining *1 tablespoon* sugar and cornstarch; stir in cranberry sauce. Spoon over cheese layer. Top with reserved crumb mixture. Bake 40 minutes or until lightly browned. Cool. Chill. Garnish as desired. Cut into bars. Store covered in refrigerator.

Makes 36 to 40 bars

EXTRA MOIST & CHUNKY BROWNIES

1 (8-ounce) package cream
  cheese, softened
1 cup sugar
1 egg
1 teaspoon vanilla extract
¾ cup all-purpose flour

1 (3⅜-ounce) package
  ROYAL® Chocolate or
  Dark 'N' Sweet Chocolate
  Pudding & Pie Filling
4 (1-ounce) semisweet
  chocolate squares,
  chopped

In large bowl, with electric mixer at high speed, beat cream cheese, sugar, egg and vanilla until smooth; blend in flour and pudding mix. Spread batter into greased 8 × 8-inch microwavable dish; sprinkle with chocolate. Shield corners of dish with foil. Microwave at HIGH (100% power) for 8 to 10 minutes or until toothpick inserted in center comes out clean, rotating dish ½ turn every 2 minutes. Cool completely in pan. Cut into squares.

Makes about 16 brownies

MINTED CHOCOLATE CHIP BROWNIES

¾ cup granulated sugar
½ cup butter or margarine
2 tablespoons water
1 cup semisweet chocolate
    chips or mini chocolate
    chips
1½ teaspoons vanilla

2 large eggs
1¼ cups all-purpose flour
½ teaspoon baking soda
½ teaspoon salt
1 cup mint chocolate chips
    Powdered sugar for garnish

Preheat oven to 350°F. Combine sugar, butter and water in medium microwavable bowl. Microwave on HIGH 2½ to 3 minutes or until butter is melted. Stir in semisweet chips; stir gently until chips are melted and mixture is well blended. Stir in vanilla; let stand 5 minutes to cool. Beat eggs into chocolate mixture, one at a time. Add combined flour, baking soda and salt; stir in mint chips. Spread into greased 9×9-inch pan.

Bake 25 minutes for fudgy brownies or 30 to 35 minutes for cakelike brownies. Remove pan to wire rack; cool completely. Cut into 2¼-inch squares. Sprinkle with powdered sugar, if desired.

Makes 16 brownies

Minted Chocolate Chip Brownies

Acknowledgments

The publishers would like to thank the companies and organizations
listed below for the use of their recipes and photographs in this publication.

American Dairy Association

Best Foods, a Division of CPC International Inc.

Borden Kitchens, Borden, Inc.

Diamond Walnut Growers, Inc.

Dole Food Company, Inc.

Hershey Foods Corporation

Kellogg Company

Kraft Foods, Inc.

Leaf,® Inc.

M&M/Mars

Nabisco Foods Group

Nestlé Food Company

New York Apple Association, Inc.

The Procter & Gamble Company

The Quaker Oats Company

Ralston Foods, Inc.

The Sugar Association, Inc.

Washington Apple Commission

Index